Darrell Dennis
Two Plays

Darrell Dennis
Two Plays

Tales of an Urban Indian

The Trickster of Third Avenue East

Playwrights Canada Press
Toronto

Darrell Dennis: Two Plays © Copyright 2005 Darrell Dennis
Tales of an Urban Indian © Copyright 2003 Darrell Dennis
The Trickster of Third Avenue East © Copyright 2000 Darrell Dennis

First edition: July 2005. Fourth printing: February 2017.
Printed and bound in Canada by Imprimerie Gauvin, Gatineau.

PLAYWRIGHTS CANADA PRESS
202-269 Richmond Street West, Toronto, ON M5V 1X1
416.703.0013 • info@playwrightscanada.com • www.playwrightscanada.com

Cover painting, *Tales of an Urban Indian*, by Luke J. Parnell
Cover design & production editing: JLArt

LIBRARY AND ARCHIVES CANADA CATALOGUING IN PUBLICATION
Dennis, Darrell (Darrell Michael)
Darrell Dennis : two plays.

Contents: The trickster of Third Avenue East -- Tales of an urban Indian.
ISBN 978-0-88754-772-0

1. Indians of North America--Canada--Drama. 2. City and town
life--Canada--Drama. I. Title. II. Title: The trickster of Third Avenue East.
III. Title: Tales of an urban Indian.

PS8607.E67D37 2005   C812'.6   C2005-903869-1

We acknowledge the financial support of the Canada Council for the Arts, the Ontario
Arts Council (OAC), the Ontario Media Development Corporation, and the Government
of Canada through the Canada Book Fund for our publishing activities.

 Canada Council
for the Arts
Conseil des arts
du Canada

 ONTARIO ARTS COUNCIL
CONSEIL DES ARTS DE L'ONTARIO
an Ontario government agency
un organisme du gouvernement de l'Ontario

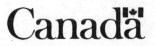 Canada

 Ontario
Ontario Media Development
Corporation

Table of Contents

Introduction
  by Lee Maracle   iii

Tales of an Urban Indian   1

The Trickster of Third Avenue East   57

Playwright's Bio   119

Introduction

by Lee Maracle

In the Coast Salish language art literally means "way of life," we are expected to live life artfully, be artistic in our approach to all aspects of our life. At the same time, there were rigorous rules applied to art within which we were expected to create. Only four shapes are used to create the carved house posts, bent boxes, and spoons and feast bowls. These four shapes are applied to a limited animal world. Yet each artist is expected to produce a unique work of art from these shapes from the very ordinary and utilitarian objects of life. We did not merely dress up, we decorated ourselves. We considered our character, our relationship to community, to one another and we sought—through dreams, through ceremony, through the reflection of the journey our lives had been personally—to decorate ourselves accordingly. From the shellfish we ate, came buttons, earrings, and necklaces. The goal of art was to reflect our personal relationship to creation and our journey through trials. We were called upon to use the waste from food consumption to create the jewellery with which we decorated ourselves and the needles, spoons, braided headdresses and so forth. The separation between life and art was always a blurry one.

Living life as art was required; our children were disciplined through the creation of story. They were educated through story, and through story they were expected to become both artists and disciplined citizens. Each one of us was to enter the adult world through song and dance, our own song and dance. Each one of us was expected to know the stories of the nation and to use those stories in their own context, to create myths from them. Interior Salish people, from whom Darrell Dennis hails, are relatives of ours. The Secwepemc people are less flamboyant than are the Coast Salish, but they are no less artistic. Word play and story mark them in much the same way. What is important is not so much the "plot" or what happened, but the response of the character in the story. What is heroic for us is not the valour of the individual, but rather the humour with which they can present the obstacles in their path and their ability to amuse themselves over their personal responses to the obstacles.

Darrell hangs from his origins by a thin thread like many young artists of today, but as the saying goes, the apple does not fall far from the tree. The creation of story from his personal journey is what *Tales of an Urban Indian* is all about. Mr. Dennis' story is not unlike the stories of many young people: he owns the resentment, the anger, the feeling of absurdity of many youth who are expected to be spiritual icons, elegant near noble savages, at the same time, young people endure very real obstacles to simple being. Disconnected from original being, we can all only imagine what it might have been like to be an "Indian" a hundred and fifty years ago, yet in the imagination of those we are surrounded by, there is an expectation that we are still prayerful and ceremonious, full of old traditions. This imagined being presents a major obstacle to young modern artists like Darrell, as a Secwepemc, Darrell is expected to create art from it in the same way his ancestors did a century and a half ago, before cultural prohibition, hunger and death plagued his people, and he does so in a way that other modern young artists are doing.

Like Margo Kane (*Moonlodge*) and Columpa Bobb (*Dinky*), Darrell Dennis is part of a new wave of performance artists who take hold of their lives, recreate their journey through it from their unique perspectives. Along the way they bust stereotypes and address tragedy, abuse of all sorts, and the attack on their individuality that stereotypes, tragedy and abuse naturally become. He rises from this journey heroic, not because he fought the "good fight" and won, but because through all of the obstacles life presents, he challenged himself and transformed in the process.

In the storytelling tradition of both Interior and Coast Salish people, we challenge our own stereotypes—not as victims who had those stereotypes foisted on ourselves, but as players on the stage of our lives that had choices and slid into the one that hurt another human being. Courage is marked not by our ability to fight the "enemy outside," but rather the "strength to fight our greatest enemy, myself" (Chief Dan George). Darrell's regret over his role in contributing to homophobic harassment reposes the highest moral standard on himself. While he did not actively make fun of this lad in the same way others did, he did not step forward either. This moment of regret is the turning point of his play, and with his life. In this moment of assuming personal responsibility for the direction of his humanity, Darrell connects himself to his Secwepemc past.

I have seen a number of "one person" shows around stereotypes and the journey of Indigenous youth through our transition from the past into the modern world. As a form it suits. First because the challenge of performing and filling a stage with a full show is connected to the challenge of creating art from a very few basic shapes. Secondly, it calls upon the performer to challenge the emotionality of those who might otherwise corral their being into a thin wedge of expectation, to transform the sort of persecution we all feel at times, into good humour and good fun. Thirdly, it provides the storyteller with the opportunity to seize a common thread, a common story line and create a new myth from it. And lastly, it presents the author of the tale to reveal their very core selves, their values, and their private world of emotions.

Darrell's play succeeds on all counts. We are moved. We are challenged. We re-experience our own journeys and realise that "oppression" itself is a modern myth. Even during the long period of cultural prohibition and removal from our communities to residential schools we had choices. As humans we are expected to find freedom in the context we inherit—no matter how terrible, conflicting or tragic the context might be. We are further called upon to make art from within our context. Darrell succeeds with grace and courage.

Our humour has its own discipline. We are called upon to laugh at our absurd responses to obstacles and transform our audience in the process. The purpose of humour is to open the audience to their own inadequacies in response to a common journey. I laughed and wept at Darrell's resentments around being expected to be culturally appropriate, at the same time as the means by which to be culturally appropriate are separated from us. Add to this, the modernity and inappropriateness of some of our cultural practices in the modern world and the resentment becomes acidic.

In the process of "storying" up his journey in dramatic performance Darrell adds something new to the existing frameworks (I resist calling it the canon) of what drama is all about. This inside peek into his responses to his personal journey transformed in a one-man show is new, but not disconnected to the performance art of young Aboriginal playwrights. What is different about this play is Darrell Dennis' courage in challenging himself in good Secwepemc fashion. If the journey is "harrowing" it is partly because Mr. Dennis made it so. Despite the difficulties his life presented, Mr. Dennis was never a victim and we all need to know that. Despite the journey, Mr. Dennis stood up and took advantage of the opportunity to strengthen his character at every turn and that is what good drama is for Salish people.

•••

Lee Maracle is a member of the Sto:lo [Coast Salish] nation. She was born in North Vancouver and is the mother of four and the grandmother of four. She is the author of a number of critically acclaimed works, including *Bobbi Lee: Indian Rebel, Ravensong, Will's Garden, Daughters are Forever, Bentbox, I Am Woman, Telling It: Women and Language Across Culture,*

Sojourners & Sundogs and the award-winning *My Home As I Remember*. She is currently First Nation's Writer In Residence at the University of Toronto.

Tales of an

Urban Indian

Acknowledgements

The author would like to thank the following organisations for their support in the creation of *Tales of an Urban Indian*: The Canada Council for the Arts, The National Arts Centre, The Gibraltar Point Centre for the Arts, and especially Native Earth Performing Arts (Yvette, Nina, Michelle, Dori, Sarah and everyone else associated).

The author would also like to thank the following people for their invaluable dramaturgical support: Herbie Barnes, Lorne Cardinal, Richard Greenblatt, Tamara Podemski, and Jean Yoon.

In addition, the author would like to acknowledge a handful of First Nations storytellers and performers that have inspired him, in one way or another, over the years: Herbie Barnes, Columpa C. Bobb, Gary Farmer, Chief Dan George, Graham Greene, Tomson Highway, Marie Clements, Margo Kane, Thomas King, Lee Maracle, Alanis Obonsawin, Jennifer Podemski, Tamara Podemski, Ian Ross, Will Sampson, Wes Studi, Drew Hayden Taylor, Tonto's Nephews, Gordon Tootoosis, The Turtle Gals, Floyd Red Crow Westerman... and once again, and most importantly, Tamara Podemski—the one to whom this play is dedicated because without her, I couldn't have told this story.

Tales of an Urban Indian was first produced by Native Earth Performing Arts at Artword Alternative, Toronto, in November 2003, with the following company:

Simon Douglas and Various   Darrell Dennis

Directed by Herbie Barnes
Set, Slide, and Costume Design by Christine Plunkett
Lighting Design by Michelle Ramsay
Sound Design and Original Music by Cathy Nosaty
Movement Coach by Tamara Podemski
Production Manager: Jacquie Carpenter
Stage Managers: April Nicole, Sarah Dalgleish
Lighting Operator: Stephanie Ruffolo
Set Construction: Jen Woodall
Crew: Johl Ringuette, Philip Adams

———

Tales of an Urban Indian was developed in part through a grant from the Canada Council for the Arts. The play was originally workshopped as part of the "Weesageechak Begins to Dance Festival" in September 2001, with Herbie Barnes under the direction of Jean Yoon.

Characters

Simon Douglas	Simon, Age 12	Mugger
Kye7e Josie*	Old Man	Muggee
Agent Williams	Simon, Age 13	Junkie
Tom	Janine	Gerald
Father Murray	Kim	Rhonda
Alistair	Martin	Director
Tina	Cody	Fluffy
Simon, Age 7	Simon, Age 15	Simon, Age 20
Nick	Announcer	Simon, Age 21
Hilda	Leon	Stranger
Simon, Age 10	Liver	Brenda's Father
Mary Anne	Mr. Britannia	Brenda's Mother
Daniel	Girl	Simon, Age 22
Moccasin Telegraph	Friendship Centre Indian	ATM
Scotty	Bartender	Operator
Morse Code	Walter	Mr. Louis
Copper	Edna	Stephanie
Becky	Simon, Age 17	God

Cast Size: One man.

*Kye7e—means "grandmother" in the Secwepemc language. The "7" denotes a quick stop in the word.

Set and Setting

Time: The play begins in 1972 and spans 22 years.

Place: Wolves Lake Reservation, British Columbia, and East Vancouver, British Columbia.

Length: A play in one act.

Tales of an Urban Indian

PROLOGUE

Lights up. The stage is empty except for a chair and a bucket of rocks. There is a projection screen upstage. SIMON DOUGLAS enters. He faces the audience, smiles, clears his throat, and then nods to the booth. Suddenly, a loud cacophony of Native drums and flute music is heard, interspersed with the cry of loons, howling of coyotes, and the jingling of Pow-Wow dancers. Stereotypical Native images are flashed on the screen.

SIMON *(to sound booth)* Thank you!

The sounds and images stop.

(to audience) Now that we got that out of our systems—let's begin. I apologise for the mystical Native soundtrack but I'm about to tell a story, and that requires a fitting Indian ceremony. Since I'm an Urban Indian I have to settle for whatever Pan-Indian imagery I can find.

Not very celestial, but it keeps me regular.... You see, I'm what's referred to as one of the "lucky ones." I wasn't forced to go to residential school. I wasn't adopted out. I never got sick from a Hudson Bay Blanket. The worst thing my Indian agent ever did was take fifteen percent commission on a theatre gig... I like concrete! I get lost when I'm in the woods. I can't shape shift. I've never had a vision. Never heard the owl call my name. And I've never cried when I saw someone litter. I can't even make it rain for God's sake! So go ahead, call me what you want: Apple. Paper Skin. Uncle Tomahawk. I've heard it all before.... Don't get me wrong! I have evolved from very deep roots, but that past is known to me only as I remember it, and not the way it probably *actually* happened. My story is based on memory so it's not entirely accurate, or fair. History never is. It's a story I need to tell, not because it's extraordinary but because it's common, too common, and it's not told enough. In many ways, it's a tale about my people, which automatically makes it a tale of survival. Of memory... I *remember* a place I *once* called "home," but even now that word tastes kind of funny. My people call it *SEKLEP TE PESELLKWE (Coyote Lake)* but missionaries renamed it "Coyote Lake Reservation Number Four." In my language, *SEKLEP TE PESELLKWE* does not mean "Coyote Lake Reservation Number Four." The elders say that when the missionaries first came to convert my people, the Coyotes would gather down in the valley by the lake and howl mournfully throughout the night. It used to scare the shit out of the missionaries.... The Coyotes don't come to howl anymore. They don't come at all. As my *Kye7e [Grandmother]* Josie used to say, "That's what happens when white people get scared. Things disappear."

Lights change.

SCENE 1: GENESIS

The word "Genesis" appears on the projection screen. Early seventies country music is heard softly in the background. SIMON becomes KYE7E JOSIE. She is swatting flies with a fly swatter and talking to her daughter-in-law, TINA.

JOSIE   Goddamned flies! *(to TINA)* Them kids never shut the door... Tina, sit down already! Move closer. Respect your elders—move closer! *(She swats TINA.)* Aaah you, Tina. Getting pregnant. Don't be getting into any more trouble now! You got enough to worry about makin' my new grandchild be born. Now, listen, I got a letter from my son. That no-good husband of yours. He says he's not comin' home for the birth.... It's my fault. I should have smacked him more when I was growin' him up. In the old days men used to be men! They took care of their families. Nowadays, women look after babies by themselves. *(beat)* You're not alone, Tina. Even without my son around, you're not alone. You're part of this family now. This community. *SWET7I? [Understand?]... Le7 [good]*.... Now listen, here's some Indian wisdom my mother told me when I was givin' birth: When you're at that white hospital in town—don't scream! That's what them white women do!

SIMON

Thanks to my *Kye7e* Josie, you could have heard a pin drop in the delivery room. Like most Indian babies I was numbered, tagged, registered with the DIA, and released back into the wild where they could track my movements. My mother gave me my Indian name... Robert. The DIA registered me as Simon Douglas. My mother knew this was going to cause problems down the road with medical funding, education funding, and tax-free smokes, so she marched down to the local branch of the DIA.

A federal logo appears on the projection screen with the words, "Department of Indian Assimilation." SIMON becomes AGENT WILLIAMS. He blows cigar smoke in TINA's face. We hear the sound of phones ringing and the ticking of typewriters.

AGENT WILLIAMS

Ma'am. I've been with the Department of Indian Affairs a long time. Since before there were Indians. *(chuckle)* Your Indian affair produced a kid, and now you're telling me you didn't name your kid Simon? It says right here in the *official* DIA registry book, sealed with the *official* stamp, of the *official* office of Prime Minister Pierre Elliott

Trudeau, right next to the *official* registry number, that your papoose's *official* name is *officially* Simon Douglas. Now *whom* am I supposed to believe? Some Indian off the street, or the Prime Minister of the great Dominion of Canada…? I don't care what his birth certificate says! Nobody calls Trudeau a liar! Get out of my cubicle or I'll have you strung up for treason!

SIMON   My father returned home shortly after I was born. Three years after I was born. He had been working as a reporter for a small Native newspaper and had just finished covering the uprising at Wounded Knee. The experience changed his life. He returned home, hell-bent on ending the North American conspiracy to rid the world of its Aboriginals.

SIMON becomes his father TOM. A picture of the American one-dollar bill appears on the screen.

TOM   Bad medicine. The government is using bad medicine against our people. They have captured our sacred eagle and are holding her captive on their evil dollar. In the eagle's talons are the fig leaf representing the black man, and thirteen arrows representing the red man. The first two slaves in the Americas. Slaves of the white man's dollars! When you cross the street, what is the symbol to "stop"? A red hand. A red hand of a red man. "Stay where you are, red man." "Don't move forward, red man." "Wait for the symbol of the man walking to tell you when to move." And what colour is he? That's right! He's white. Do you understand what I'm saying son?

SIMON   I was three years old! It didn't take long before he was gone again. It turned out that he had a baby on the way somewhere in the American midwest. Apparently, my father's mission was to single-handedly replenish the Indian Nation. So, in a deliberate act of revenge, my mother had me baptised. I was dumped off at the reservation church:

"Our Lady of the Converted Heathen," and placed in the stigmata hands of Father Murray.

> *SIMON becomes FATHER MURRAY. Piano music starts to play. Cabaret lighting comes up.*

FATHER MURRAY   Hello there little boy, and welcome to your new home. Comfy? Of course you are. It's always room temperature in the house of the Lord. Your mother did the right thing by bringing you here. This is salvation, boy. This is your way station to paradise. *this...* is where the magic happens!

(singing) Before Columbus found this placeYour people were a savage raceYou crawled around on hands and kneesAte rocks and dirt and swung from trees

So we traded bibles for your heathen soulsAnd burned down all your totem polesBut you still denied our saviours rulesSo we sent you all to boarding schools

And what thanks did we receiveStill so many don't believeYou returned to your godless smudge and drumAnd tossed away our trader's rum

> *Crescendo.*

But remember as you sit in your sweatSplashing water on the rocksIf God had wanted you to pray that wayHe wouldn't have created smaaall POX!

(to SIMON, spoken) Now hold your breath boy, and start renouncing Satan!

> *He pushes SIMON under the water. We hear the sound of bubbles. Lights change.*

SCENE 2: COYOTE LAKE

	The words "Coyote Lake" appear on the projection screen. They are replaced by pictures of reservation Indian children at play.
SIMON	Our reserve was smack dab in the middle of a semi-arid desert, but when summer rolled around there was nothing *semi*-arid about the place. It was a heaping helping' of arid with a side order of goddamn it's hot! To cool off I went swimming down at the lake, with my buddies Nick and Daniel. Afterwards we would towel off and pull the leeches off each other. For some reason, Daniel's hands always seemed to linger just a little bit longer on our backs... I was a happy, well-adjusted, seven-year-old Native child, so naturally I had to be removed from my community.... My mother was working at a restaurant in town that boasted authentic Chinese and Canadian cuisine. She had just served her eighteenth shrimp fried rice, when in walked ALISTAIR—a Marxist-Leninist, pseudo-Anarchist, Lacto-Ovo-Vegetarian, tree-planter. The moment Alistair saw Tina; he fell head over heels in love with her status card. Finally, after two months of dating, Alistair made the hour-long drive, over dusty gravel roads, to meet the family.... Guess who's coming to dinner?
	SIMON becomes ALISTAIR.
ALISTAIR	Oh, no thank you, Josie. I can't bear to eat these processed meats and canned foods. I'm a macro-biotic. You know, if Natives implemented a gardening co-operative it would really cut down on the obesity in their communities. Did I say Native?—I meant Aboriginal. I try to use correct terminology in referring to people of pigment! Which reminds me... Tina and I have been discussing Simon's future. We feel that his development would best be served in a more progressive, multicultural environment. So the three of us are

moving to Vancouver! Isn't that exciting…?! Pass the yams please.

KYE7E JOSIE passes the yams. Stunned.

JOSIE   Tina, is this true?

ALISTAIR   Tina feels that she doesn't belong here. She's from a different reservation. She wants something better for herself, and for Simon.

JOSIE   *(to ALISTAIR)* Fancy man! I'm talking to Tina. *(to TINA)* Tina, is this what you really want? Tell me the truth. You're my daughter.

TINA   I'm your daughter-in-law. This isn't even my reserve. If Simon stays here, he's just going to end up a drunk!

JOSIE   *(hurt)* After all this time, that's all you've seen, eh? I hope you'll be happy there.

TINA   Kye7e, I have no choice!

JOSIE   Choice is the only thing you never lose.

JOSIE exits.

SIMON   Like a miracle, my father came back to the reserve. He was staying at his brother's house and he was just going to be there one night. I was leaving for the city the next day, so I had to act fast. I packed my knapsack full of soups and tins of Spork, then sent for my trusted buddy, Nick.

NICK arrives munching on something.

NICK   Sorry I took so long. I was eating breakfast. Then I got hungry again. So I had some lunch. It was really good!

SIMON, AGE 7   God, Nick! You're always eating! My Kye7e says you got a tapeworm.

NICK   It's not a tapeworm! My mom says I got good metal-bowl-ism!

SIMON, AGE 7   Never mind that! I need you to do something important Nick. Go find my dad. Tell him my mom's forcing me to go live in the city. Tell him they're going to bleach my skin and call me Stuart, or something *white* like that. Tell him I want to go around the country with him and sleep in tee-pees, and shoot bows and arrows, and fight cowboys.... Hurry Nick! Tell him before it's too late!

NICK   Okay, I'll tell him...! You going to eat that tin of Spork?

SIMON   I sat and waited by the window for my father to come and rescue me... and waited...

SIMON, AGE 7 falls asleep.

When I woke up the next morning, my Kye7e was just sitting there, staring out the window. She knew what had happened—I don't know how—but she always knew.

JOSIE   It's not your fault, Simon. It's not *his* fault. They took him. They put him in a truck, and dumped him off like garbage at the residential school. They said they'd teach him how to be welcome in their world. But they didn't teach him nothing. Just hate. Don't think your father doesn't care, Simon. He just forgot how to love. *(beat)* Gimme me your hand. Inside this can is a piece of your land. Your home. Never forget you have a home.

She places a small, plastic film container in SIMON's hand.

SIMON   *(beat)* And we were gone.

SIMON places the container at the front of the stage. Lights change.

SCENE 3: LOTUS LAND

	The words "Lotus Land" appear on the projection screen. They are replaced by a panoramic view of Vancouver. City sounds and 70s rock music is heard.
SIMON	East Vancouver, British Columbia. The big bowl of granola. Full of nuts, fruits, and flakes. We moved into the basement of Alistair's mother's house. She was an older German woman whose hair was pulled back so tight she could taste the back of her head. From the moment we arrived, she started to civilise us.
HILDA	*(thick German accent) Achtung*, Indianer! You vill remove your filthy elbows from ze dinner table immediately. Sit up straight! Ze small fork is for ze salad! Big fork for ze schnitzel! Eat, *meine klein hund!* Schnell! Schnell!—Aha! Was ist das? It vould appear zat you have dropped your napkin— you naughty kitten—now you shall have no pie.
SIMON	Every child rebels against its parent's fascist dictatorship and Alistair was no exception. He ensured that the entire house was steeped in a quagmire of political correctness. For three years, no matter what we said or did, it could always be more "progressive."
SIMON, AGE 10	Alistair! Alistair! Look what I did at school! It's a picture of a black horse and it's under a big yellow sun with a smiling face—
ALISTAIR	Simon, don't say *black*, that's racist, say *shaded*. And don't say *yellow*, say *Asian*.
SIMON, AGE 10	But it's not an Asian. It's the sun.
ALISTAIR	Where are the daughters? That's patriarchal. From now on you are only to draw women of colour who dominate subservient men. If you could also draw them in a healthy lesbian relationship, that would be very empowering.

SIMON	For my birthday I asked for "Monopoly" and instead I got "cooperative games." Alistair's mother would lock herself in her room all day and all night listening to old German marching records. No music, just the sound of boots. Since Alistair had free reign of the house, there was always a party going on. My clothes smelled of cigarettes and pot and my schoolbooks reeked of beer. So, in trying to save us from Indian alcohol abuse, my mother placed us right in the middle of white alcohol abuse. The only difference was white people called it "blowing off a little steam." My mother's job at the parties was to set out the food, which always drew a crowd of Alistair's friends.
MARY ANNE	Tina, this food looks delicious. What kind of berries are those?
TINA	Straw.
MARY ANNE	Where did you pick them?
TINA	Safeway.
MARY ANNE	And this meat: Moose? Venison?
TINA	Hamburger. Hot dog.
MARY ANNE	(emotional) Thank you, Tina…. Thank you.
SIMON	It didn't take long for my mother to feel like she was on display. She was miserable, so she started drinking a lot. It became obvious to Alistair that "the Native was getting restless."
ALISTAIR	Tina, I respect you on so many levels. As my lover, as a woman of colour, and as an equal, but lately, your behaviour and appearance have been somewhat jarring. Your beautiful red complexion is turning an off-yellow colour—
SIMON, AGE 10	Um… Asian.
ALISTAIR	Thank you Simon—and your wardrobe has become so urban and cliché. It's like you're trying to assimilate. All I've seen from you is the pursuit of instant gratification. Not very Aboriginal, Tina.

I never thought I'd say this, but I'm very disappointed in you.

TINA   *(pause, fuming) EXCUSE ME!?*

A crack of thunder is heard.

SIMON   Alistair and I both learned a valuable lesson that day. Native women will put up with centuries worth of shit. But they have a breaking point, and if your Native woman starts a sentence with the words, *"EXCUSE ME!?"—RUN!*

TINA   You're disappointed!? How am I supposed to look? You want me in a little buckskin mini skirt!? Wearing furs? My hair in braids? You met me a little too late Alistair. You would have loved me back in the sixteen-hundreds! You don't want a real Indian woman; you want some primitive sexual fantasy. Well I ain't acting like Pocahontas for you, 'cause the only thing she got from her white man was dead. All you do is drink and smoke up, but when I want to join the party you turn into Bill W. You condescending, racist, hypocrite! Simon and I aren't little Indian dolls you show off to your friends. I don't act Indian, because I *am* Indian! This is what we are Alistair. This is what we've become. Deal with it! We live in a city, for Christ sake! How do you expect me to get close to Mother Earth! SHE'S COVERED IN FUCKING CONCRETE, YOU ASSHOLE!!

SIMON   That was the first and last time my mother was accused of being an Indian princess. After three blurry years, we were finally going home.

        Lights change.

Scene 4: New Beginnings

	The words, "New Beginnings" are shown on the projection screen.
SIMON	Most people on my reserve had no regular contact with white people so everybody wanted to hear about my adventures in Wonderbread land, especially Nick and Daniel. I was like Christopher Columbus, only in reverse. The first few weeks I was back, I became a ten-year-old tribal storyteller.
NICK	Simon! Simon! Tell us again about the white people!
SIMON, AGE 10	When white people are eating dinner and you stop by for a visit, they don't put out a plate for you, they ask you to come back later.
DANIEL	Ooooh...
SIMON, AGE 10	When white people drink beer they say stuff like "I love you, man" and "nobody at the office knows how hard I work."
NICK	Aaaaah...
SIMON, AGE 10	White people can go through their whole lives living next door to someone, and never crash out on their neighbours couch.
NICK	Ohhhhh...
DANIEL	Impossible...
NICK	Unbelievable...
DANIEL	Noooo...!
SIMON	Now every family has that one relative that proves we evolved from apes. My family had cousin Scotty. He was known as an FBI—Fuckin' Big Indian! He was the popular kid on the reserve, because everybody was scared of him. No one ever wanted to get on his bad side. Unfortunately, I did. With a little help from the *Moccasin Telegraph*.

MOCCASIN TELEGRAPH	Pssst, did you hear? Scotty's girlfriend Suzy has a crush on Simon Douglas.... Pssst, did you hear? Scotty's girlfriend Suzy showed her bust to Simon Douglas.... Pssst, did you hear? Scotty's mule friend was woozy in the dust, now its hymen is bugless...
SIMON	Scotty wanted revenge, but instead of beating me squishy, he went for the jugular and spread the most damaging rumour that could ever be spread about a reserve boy.
SCOTTY	Pssst... Simon's gay. No, not happy gay. A ho-mo. What do you expect? He lived in the city.
SIMON	Word spread like wildfire.
MORSE CODE	*(tapping out message)* Mayday, mayday. Simon's gay, Simon's gay!
COPPER	*(into PA)* Calling all cars, calling all cars. Be on the lookout for Simon Douglas. He's considered armed and very gay.

> *SIMON does Semaphore signals and ends it with a limp wrist.*

SIMON	So for the next two years I had to prove my manhood. I needed a girlfriend but it was hard to find one that I wasn't related to. So, I started "going around" with Becky. She was an exact carbon copy of the rest of the girls on the reserve: easily embarrassed, hands hidden in her jacket sleeves, mouth covered when she spoke. And she spoke in a language called *reservism*...
BECKY	Ever dumb you! Sick! Koh! Nyahhh! Gwan! Neeeh! As if! Aaaiii...!
SIMON	I held hands with her wherever we went. I also started to display my medals of honour, commonly awarded to reserve boys: The purple badges of Hickeydom. At last, I was cleared of all gay charges.... That's when my relationship with Daniel became problematic. Growing up, Daniel

was a little more gentle than the rest of us. I could say anything to him. Whenever I talked about how I was feeling, he never laughed or made fun like all the other kids. He just smiled and said, "I understand." As little kids, Daniel would put on his mom's apron and make mud pies for us. Nick would eat the mud pies, rocks and all. When we got older, the three of us built a tree fort. Daniel decorated it. Nick ate all the wood-chips because he only heard the chip part. We made a great trio, Daniel Nick, and I. But there comes a point in every boy's life when he must choose the allegiances that define him till the day he dies. Daniel's softness wasn't complimentary anymore, it was dangerous. Just like that, my reputation was threatened again. Even Nick started to worry about me.

NICK
(eating chips) You know Simon, when Scotty was telling everyone you were a fag, I never believed him. But you been hanging around with Daniel a lot lately, and you know the saying, "Fool me once, shame on you. Fool me twice—you're a fag."

SIMON
The thing about our reserve was that everyone professed to hating fags, but when it came to Daniel, everybody just sort of tolerated him. Partly because he was related to half the reserve and partly because everyone just thought he'd grow out of it. But when Daniel got older, his increasing gentleness became increasingly more threatening. I had to distance myself. So whenever Daniel was around I'd say...

SIMON, AGE 12
Hey, look who's here; it's Daniel the Butt Pony. You come lookin' for your rump jockey? Why don't you go put on a saddle and.... Get ridden... like a... horse... and.... Uh.... Fag!

SIMON
Then, I bounced a pop can off his head. It wasn't clever, but at least I made my point—*I was the Anti-Fag!*... After a while, I became immune to the hurt in his eyes as he crawled home.

The sound of church bells is heard.

Daniel hadn't come home for two nights and nobody knew where he was. His family searched everywhere, even the surrounding hillside. On the third morning, Daniel's father woke up with a strong impulse to go for a walk. He took the dog and walked deep into the woods behind the reserve. As he pushed his way through the thick brush, the dog froze. Up in the distance was Daniel, naked, and dangling from a tree... I didn't go to the funeral. Not many of us did. Days later as Daniel's mother was cleaning up his room, she found the suicide note that had somehow fallen behind the bed. The *Moccasin Telegraph* swept through the reserve and before the day was out everybody knew verbatim what it said.

(as DANIEL) "I can't take it anymore. I can't take the way people look at me, or what they say. I know they think I'm weird for how I feel but I can't help it, I didn't ask to be born this way. Tell all those people who hated me or who I made feel ugly, that I'm sorry."

> *SIMON goes to the bucket and places a rock at the front of the stage.*

On reserves, a suicide always causes a domino effect. As it turns out, our other friend Lisa wasn't just a tomboy like we all thought. Right after Daniel's death, Lisa got drunk and locked herself in a room with a rifle. That room is now permanently locked.

> *SIMON places a second rock at the front of the stage. The low murmur of biblical readings is heard.*

At Lisa's funeral, I watched my Kye7e Josie speak to an old man in a dirty cowboy hat, with a ragged eagle feather stuck in the band.

JOSIE	There was a time when two-spirited people of this village were honoured. They were respected for possessing both sexes.
OLD MAN	Aaaah, no! They disrespected the creator. If they had prayed more, or went to the sweat lodge, they could have cured themselves of being gay.
SIMON	At that moment I started to realise the difference between being an elder, and just being old.

Lights change.

SCENE 5: GIRLS, GIRLS, GIRLS

	The words "Girls, Girls, Girls" appear on the projection screen. "Girls, Girls, Girls" by Mötley Crüe is heard.
SIMON	For some of us, life goes on. I was now blossoming into a thirteen-year-old and that meant one thing: Girls! Whenever night fell on the reserve, all the young people would come out of their homes to prowl the dusty roads. There was toking and drinking and the always-hopeful promise of S-E-X. Everyone was doing it—except for me. Becky didn't want to be around me anymore because I had suddenly become immature. As it turns out, teenage boys have to take what they can get, but teenage girls can get what they want. And Becky could get more than a thirteen-year-old boy. That's when Janine came to the reserve to stay with her uncle. She had run into some trouble of an undisclosed nature on her own reserve. She showed up wearing heavy makeup, a low-cut blouse, and a high-cut skirt. She had those long legs that went all the way up and made an ass of themselves. And us. A girl destined to develop a reputation.

SIMON, AGE 13	Hey Janine! You got any Indian in 'ya? Want some? Ha Ha Ha Ha! Go Nick.
NICK	Janine, you wanna play a game of hide the salami? Ha Ha Ha! *(to himself)* Man, I'm hungry…. Go Simon!
SIMON, AGE 13	Hey Janine! Why don't I make a deposit in your beaver bank? Ha Ha Ha—!
JANINE	Okay…. What are you standing there bug-eyed for? I know you want me. I know these girls 'round here don't give you any. That's why they're all jealous of me. All the boys here only want me. You want me, right? I know you do. You all want this body. If all I gotta do is give this out for a few minutes, then so what? It's just a body, right? So are we going to do this, or what?
SIMON, AGE 13	Um… I just remembered, I got something to do… *(to NICK)* Run!
SIMON	But it was no use. With her gazelle-like legs, she leaped over the band office in a single bound and grabbed us by the scruff of our necks. That night the two of us took turns in the basement of the community hall. A week later she was gone. Nobody asked where she was or even mentioned her name.
	Lights change.

Scene 6: Forbidden Fruit

	The words "Forbidden Fruit" appear on the projection screen.
SIMON	By the start of the eighth grade I was catching the bus to attend junior high. It would get to the reserve at 7:30 a.m., and for about an hour there was fun for Natives of all ages. Then the bus would arrive in town and we would pull into the golf

course where the rich white kids lived. All the Natives would fall silent and move to the back of the bus. If you listened closely, you could hear Rosa Parks cussing us out. Then, a sea of blonde hair, designer clothes, and an overpowering smell of perfume would flood the bus. The master race. Any brown person trapped in a seat beside a white person was the focus of the tribe.

NICK

Tommy's in a window seat beside a white one!

SIMON, AGE 13

You stay here. I'm going in to get him.

NICK

For the love of God, man. No sudden movements. They can smell fear.

SIMON, AGE 13

Dammit! We got Math together. I'm not leaving him behind.

SIMON

It was us against them, even though none of them knew we existed. Except when they had to sit beside one of us. They would turn up their noses and roll their eyes. When we finally got to school it was just more of the same. Indians against whites. Rich against poor. Everybody against the East Indians. You could walk from one end of the hall to the next and hear all the nations of the world slammed between periods. "Honky" "Wagon-burner" "Chink" "Packie" "Wop" "Kike" "Spade." Everyone stayed with their own, the status quo was maintained, and everybody was expected to be content. That's when I started to crave the forbidden fruit. The white girls at my school seemed so pure. They didn't walk down the hall, they floated, and little cartoon animals would flock around them. They had it all. They were living the life we saw on TV. Where every problem was solved in twenty-two minutes. The apple of my eye was Kimberly Thompson. She had big, pouty lips, she wore an adult-sized bra, and she came from Viking stock. I found her name in the phonebook and with my best pal Nick beside me, I was about to break on through to the other side... I dialled the number. My heart was pounding through my chest. My face was burning. Nick was standing in front of me, breathing his beef jerky breath in my face. One ring. "Oh God, please don't be home." Two rings. "Please God, don't let her be home." Three rings. "Thank you, God." Click.

KIM	Hello?
SIMON, AGE 13	Uh.... Hi. Is this Kim? This is Simon. I sit three seats behind you in Social Studies. One row over.
KIM	Oh, hi! How was your track meet?
SIMON, AGE 13	I'm not in track. Do you like track? I could be in track.
KIM	You're not the blond guy, who always wears the green leather jacket?
SIMON, AGE 13	No. I'm the Indian guy who always wears the black Rugby pants. They're the only pants I got. *(hitting himself on his head)* Stupid, stupid, stupid. *(back into phone)* So, Kim, I was wondering if you would like to go out sometime? I live on the Coyote Lake Reserve. It's about an hour out of town, but my mom could drive me in—
KIM	Listen Simon, you sound like a really nice guy, and I think it's real cute that you asked me out—*but*—
SIMON	I've heard the word "but" a million times after this phone call and it never gets easier.
KIM	—*But*—and don't be offended by this—*but*— you're Indian. Why don't you ask out one of the girls on your reserve? There must be plenty of them that would love a chance to date you.
SIMON, AGE 13	Yeah, thanks. I'll consider it.

He hangs up the phone.

NICK	So? Is she going to play "Simon sez?" What happened man?
SIMON, AGE 13	She doesn't want to go out with no reserve Indian, that's what happened. Can you blame her? These white girls get on our bus and there's

chewing-tobacco spit on the floor, our girls are all pregnant, we talk funny, our clothes are from the seventies, and were all broke. We're supposed to be close to nature and all you see around here is garbage on the roads and broken-down fridges in our yards. People here always say they're proud to be Indian, but what the fuck is there to be proud of? No wonder white people always make fun of us. It's a fucking disgrace! I wouldn't want to go out with me either!

NICK   Ohhh…. Wanna go to the store and buy some more chips?

SIMON, AGE 13   No! I'm going to my room to brood.

> *SIMON slams his bedroom door and hits Play on his boom box. "Broken Wings" by Mr. Mister, is heard. SIMON sings along passionately.*

From this moment on, things are going to change! You hear me world?! Things are going to change!!

> *Music stops. Lights change.*

Scene 7: New Identity

> *The words "New Identity" appear on the projection screen.*

SIMON   It was clear that I wasn't going to get ahead in life as an Indian. What I really wanted was to leave the reserve, but failing that I had to set myself apart from the others. I wasn't athletic, so all that was left was class clown. Most of my material was just regurgitated "Saturday Night Live" and "SCTV" re-runs. The students loved it. The teachers…?

> *We hear muted trombone sounds that indicate teachers speaking. Just like the "Peanuts" cartoon.*

SIMON, AGE 13	What's that, ma'am...? Go to the office...? Good grief!
SIMON	I was getting into a lot of trouble so the school counsellors enrolled me in the Drama program. Acting as a form of Ritalin. This was it! My ticket to popularity! My name in lights, tawdry affairs with leading ladies, Simon Douglas action figures with Kung Fu grip...! I walked into the drama portable and there in front of me were pimply-faced boys, playing Dungeons and Dragons and misquoting Monty Python. To make matters worse, I was the only Native in the entire history of the school to take Drama. Despite my bush Indian accent and circa 1975 Buster Brown shoes, I was cast in the school play as a charming, playboy lady-killer. The moment I stepped on stage, I started to convulse. The Kool-Aid kept shaking out of the wine glass I was holding. I struggled through until the last ten minutes of the play, and just as I was about to deliver my final speech:

> *Spotlight. SIMON freezes. Sound of heartbeat. The heartbeat flat lines. Long uncomfortable pause.*

Panic stricken, I turned to my scene partner for help!

> *He imitates scene partner who is ignoring him. She is filing her nails.*

Finally, the play ended to a light smattering of applause. I went backstage and threw up for an hour. It was exhilarating! This was my calling! I couldn't wait to tell Nick and my other buddies, Martin and Cody, about my new identity. I had a title now. Simon Douglas—Thespian!

MARTIN	*(laughing)* A lesbian!?
CODY	Where are you going to act on the reserve? You're going to be poorer than my cousin Alfie and he's on welfare.

SIMON	Then I noticed, Nick wasn't laughing.
NICK	What the hell's so funny? At least Simon's doing something. Even if he's bad at it—and believe me, I saw the play—he's really bad. But at least he's doing something.
SIMON, AGE 13	Naw, that's cool, Nick. They're right. There ain't no Indian actors. Just that guy on Beachcombers. How am I supposed to make money?
NICK	Fuck money! Who's gonna hire us anyway? People always think we're gonna show up drunk or not show up at all. We're going to be broke anyway. You might as well be poor doing something you like.
SIMON	That was Nick's way of saying he believed in me. And you know what? The guys actually backed off. Not because they believed in me too, but because they all knew what Nick said was true. When you're at the bottom, anything is moving up.
SIMON, AGE 13	Thanks Nick.
NICK	(beat, awkward) Doesn't mean we're engaged or nothing!
	Lights change.

SCENE 8: LIQUOR IS QUICKER

	The words "Liquor Is Quicker" appear on the projection screen.
SIMON	At fifteen, I had yet to repeat my first sexual encounter. Kimberly's rejection did a number on my self-esteem. So, I was forced to seek out my courage the old fashioned way.... The first time I got drunk, was with Nick. We sat behind the church and chugged back a huge bottle of whiskey. I was indestructible. I was James Bond. Suave and

	de-boner. The ladies were powerless around my rapier wit.
SIMON, AGE 15	*(à la Sean Connery)* Excuse me ladies, I wish to inform you that there's a party in my pants and I want you all to come.
SIMON	At least that's what I heard myself say. To the ladies it went a little something like this:
SIMON, AGE 15	Hey!! You wansa come for to pie and doopy woopy gaga moo moo...
SIMON	Something was churning in my stomach. I was experiencing a wooziness I had never felt before.

Sound of boxing bell ringing.

ANNOUNCER	And that bell signals the first round between Simon's stomach and gravity. This is Simon's first professional fight in the whiskey arena and already he seems to be buckling. Uh oh! Large pools of saliva are forming in his mouth. Leon, what should Simon be doing at this point?
LEON	Back in '74, I had trouble with spit mouth during my title bout with Jägermeister. Simon is going to have to use the flexibility he displayed earlier on, to bend over and kiss his ass goodbye.
ANNOUNCER	Joining us now at ringside is Simon's liver. Simon's liver, what do you think his chances are tonight?
LIVER	If Simon wins this one, I'm next in line for a title shot. I'm gonna get bigger and bigger and bigger until I explode! Whatcha gonna do Simon? Whatcha gonna do when Sclerosis Mania runs wild on you!!
ANNOUNCER	Uh-oh. Simon's down on his knees and—is he? Yes folks, he's doing the Technicolour yawn. Gravity wins this one. Here comes his lungs, his intestines, his kidneys—
LEON	That's all right. That stuff just grows right back.

ANNOUNCER   —And now he's puking up blood, folks. Don't
count Simon Douglas out though. I have a feeling
were going to be seeing *a lot* more of him in the
future.

Sound of boxing bell ringing madly.

SIMON   I quit drinking after that. For about a week. I just
couldn't stay away from the magic elixir. It made
me someone else. It didn't matter who, as long
as it wasn't me. Since we were now official party
dudes, Nick and I started hanging out with a much
older crowd. Like Gordon: The chief's son. On our
reserve, being the chief's son was like being the
preacher's daughter. They're both really good at
being bad. Gordon was going on a five-hour road
trip to register for classes at some community col-
lege. He invited the two of us to tag along.

SIMON, AGE 15   *(practicing)* Okay, what if I try this… Mom,
Gordon is nineteen. He's old enough to vote. He's
old enough to buy beer even—no, wait, that won't
work…. Okay, how about this…. Mom, I'm not
a little kid anymore, I'm fifteen. I'm old enough
to do adult things. You were fifteen when you got
pregnant with me—Woah! Scratch that! Wait a
minute…

SIMON thinks for a moment. Goes to TINA.

Uh, mother dear…? Uncle Charlie told me he was
going to camp out by the river tonight and do
some fishing. May I go camp with Uncle Charlie
tonight and do some fishing…? Yeah!?

SIMON   Why didn't I think of it sooner? Lying was great!
You just make something up and you get to do
stuff! Why wasn't everybody doing it?

The sound of driving is heard.

Gordon was driving. Nick was the co-pilot. We
were like Voyageurs, exploring the open frontier.
Our cargo was two cases of beer, a Mickey of

Vodka, and a bag of weed. The windows were wide open, the tunes were blasting—

"Here I Go Again" by Whitesnake is heard.

It's starting to get dark. We're getting very drunk. The speedometer's getting higher and higher. We roll up a joint. We get higher and higher. We're passing every car we come roaring up behind. Whipping in and out of traffic. We run over a porcupine—

NICK   Woah! Bad sign man.

SIMON   At about 2:00 a.m., and three quarters of the way to our destination, Nick falls asleep, then me… and then Gordon.

                 The loud sound of screeching tires is heard.

SIMON, AGE 15   Fuck, Gordon! Watch out!

                 SIMON contorts his body to match the description of the following scene.

SIMON   The road is racing up beside me. Reflector posts are slamming against my side of the truck. Glass is exploding around me. The truck flies through air and starts to roll. Once, twice, Nick is thrown into the back seat on top of me. Three times—metal is twisting and snapping. Finally, the truck comes to a crashing halt. The cabin is filled with dust. There is a long silence. "Is everybody okay?" "Yeah, I'm okay!" It was Gordon. Nick, you okay? Nick? Nick!?" *(beat)* Nick was slumped over, his head between his knees.

NICK   *(sitting up)* Yeah, Simon. Just fuckin' ducky.

SIMON   My mother drove three hours to pick us up at the RCMP detachment. She didn't say a word the whole way back. When we finally arrived at home, she said:

TINA   Start packing. We're getting out of here.

SIMON	I couldn't believe it. This was exactly what I wanted. I messed up and only good came from it. My whole concept of right and wrong, good and evil, chicken and egg was thrown into a tailspin. I stumbled into our house. Kye7e was waiting for me, gripping her fly swatter of fury. I could imagine what was going to happen next.
SIMON, AGE 15	*(holds up hands)* Ow-wie! Ow-which! Ow-wah! Ow! Ow! Uncle! Uncle!!
SIMON	But nothing happened. Kye7e was just staring at me. Then, she slowly shook her head, and walked away. It was the worst thing anyone ever didn't say to me. I just stood there and watched her shuffle into her bedroom, and then close the door.

> *SIMON places a third rock at the front of the stage.*

A couple of days later our pickup truck was loaded to the sky. Somehow, the memory of my first city experience had faded with time and ambition. All I knew now was that I was going to be more than just a reserve Indian. I was going to the city, where a man was not judged by race, creed, or colour. Where the streets were paved with gold. The last stop before greatness was Nick's house.

SIMON, AGE 15	This is it, man… so… I… you know.
NICK	Yeah. Me too.
SIMON, AGE 15	I'll come back and see you real soon, Nick.
NICK	I'll be right here buddy. I ain't going nowhere.

> *Lights change.*

SCENE 9: LOTUS LAND II

	The words "Lotus Land II" appear on the projection screen. They are replaced by the words, "This time it's personal!" This is replaced by a panoramic view of Vancouver. Hip-Hop music and other assorted city sounds are heard.
SIMON	The prodigal son returns. The moment we arrived in the melting pot I knew I was going to rise to the top. I was feeling *VERY CREAMY*! I went to meet my academic counsellor to sign up for my new courses. I'd forgotten how foreign the west coast really was.
	Simon becomes MR. BRITANNIA.
MR. BRITANNIA	Welcome to *Van-cue-ver* Simon. I'm your academic *council-leur*, Mr. Britannia, but you can just call me "dude." Sorry to keep you waiting. I was getting an estimate for some work I'm having done on my *bong*. Now it says in your transcripts that you've never taken a French course. Is that right? Damn straight! It's called *BRITISH* Columbia for a reason, am I right? High five…! So what elective courses are you interested in taking? Hydroponics, hacky sack, the Hibachi Arts…? Dude, I got the munchies. Let's go to the cafeteria. The Starbucks' kiosk serves a wicked Mochachino.
SIMON	The school was massive, and not a single Indian to be found. So I knew the girls would find me exotic. I went straight for the most popular girl in school, 'cause I was feeling particularly stupid that day. She was so beautiful. Her skin was that colour you can only get at tanning parlours: pumpkin orange! Like a wolverine, I pounced!
SIMON, AGE 15	Hey ladies! Tell me something, is it hot in here or is it just you? My name is tall, dark, and handsome. What's yours?
GIRL	Hi there, my name is *Yeah Right, As If,* and these are my friends: *Too Good For You, Not In*

A Million Years, and my baby sister *Way Out Of Your League.* Oh look, here comes my boyfriend *Tear You A New Asshole.*

SIMON
I was having a tough time fitting in. I missed Nick. I was even starting to feel a little homesick. So, I went to a dance at the Native Friendship Centre. Ironically, the Natives at the friendship centre weren't very friendly.

INDIAN
What nation you from? *Secwepemc (Shuswap)?* Goddamned Interior Salish. This is the Haida section. Go stand over there in the Cree section. The bathroom is over there, between the Thompson section and the Blackfoot section. Don't use the first two urinals. Those belong to the Okanagans and the Carriers. Now get out of here, before I bannock slap you! *G'WAN!*

SIMON
I wandered the streets of Vancouver, looking for anybody I could relate to. Then, I turned a corner and found myself standing on *Hastings Street!*

"O Fortuna" is heard. A picture of Hastings Street at night is shown on the projection screen.

The Street was a shimmering kingdom of neon. There were Natives everywhere. Everybody knew each other. And they were so friendly. They kept asking me if I needed anything? If I was looking for anything? If I had anything? I felt like I had walked into a Broadway musical, and everything was coming up roses... I eventually found myself in a seedy little dive.

BARTENDER
You nineteen?

SIMON, AGE 15
If I wasn't nineteen, would I be in a bar?

BARTENDER
You raise an interesting point. One beer coming up.

SIMON
This was awesome! They were serving me booze and I was only fifteen years old. I turned, and high-fived the thirteen-year-old at the next table. Five hours and six pitchers of beer later, I tried

to leave but was stopped by my new best friend, Walter.

The sound of clinking glass, old time rock and roll, and bar atmosphere. SIMON becomes WALTER.

WALTER: Naw, Simon. Stay for one more round. You gotta meet my wife, Edna.... Hey Edna! Come here and meet Simon... he's from your area... up north.

EDNA: Jesus Christ, Walter! Every Indian in this bar is from up North. It's the only direction in Canada you can go from Vancouver...

SIMON: Walter and Edna had been on Hastings Street for twenty years. The fact that they were still alive made them legends. Everywhere was drinking, and laughing, and hand-shaking, and backslapping. This was what I was looking for! Good old fashioned, Indian camaraderie. The party moved over to one of the welfare hotels on the strip. That's where I stayed until 6:00 a.m. Then, the needles came out.

WALTER: Here you go Simon. I got an extra rig for 'ya.

SIMON, AGE 15: No thanks guys. I'm not really good with sharp pointy things. I'll see you later, okay?

SIMON: I'd never seen anybody shoot up before, and I wasn't going to start now. Somehow, I managed to stumble home and fall asleep. An hour later, my mother knocked on the door.

TINA: Simon?

SIMON: I was expecting the ragging out of my life. Instead...

TINA sits at the edge of SIMON's bed.

TINA: We got a call from the reserve when you were sleeping. Nick died last night. He was drinking pretty heavy. He passed out and suffocated on his own vomit.

> *SIMON places a fourth rock at the front of the stage.*

SIMON   Two days later, I was back on the reserve watching Nick's casket being lowered into the ground. Tears came pouring out of me. I cried non-stop for the rest of the day. I went out drinking that night to toast the passing of my best friend and recent statistic. I'd like to say Nick would have wanted it that way, but I'm pretty sure he would've kicked my ass.

> *Lights change.*

Scene 10: Red Power

> *The words "Red Power" appear on the projection screen.*

SIMON   I was now seventeen and completely alone, so I threw myself into school, and the endless quest for popularity. Through a steady regime of Indian denial, I actually started to make friends. To show that I was one of the boys, my friends made a point of talking in a degrading Indian accent and calling me Chief to prove that they weren't racist. Most of them associated Indians with drunks on the street so I did everything to be the opposite of their stereotype. With my developing powers of mimicry I finally managed to shake my reserve accent, sometimes going a little overboard.

SIMON, AGE 17   *(very Caucasian)* Golly gee, fellas. That sure was one humdinger of a picture show. Say here's a swell idea, why don't we skip back to my bungalow for some mayonnaise sandwiches and some Tang? I got the new Celine Dion album.

SIMON   Pretty soon my new friends actually started to believe that I was just well-tanned. After Nick's death I had gone back to Hastings Street a number of times to drown my sorrows. I could switch at the drop of a hat.

SIMON, AGE 17   *(street Indian)* Yo man. That fuckin' movie fuckin' sucked! Let's fuckin' shoot back to my fuckin' room and get fucked up! Fuckity, Fuck, Fuckin', Fuck. I got the new Celine Dion album.

SIMON   It was hard to separate the two. I was living a double life. Like Grey Owl, only in reverse. Suddenly, like a thunderbolt, the 1990s happened.

1990s contemporary Native music is heard.

The redskin renaissance! "Dances with Wolves" was a huge hit. Graham Greene was nominated for an Oscar. Robbie Robertson and Buffy Sainte-Marie were making comebacks. Elijah Harper held up an eagle feather and stopped The Meech Lake Accord. "North of 60." "Northern Exposure." "Dance Me Outside." "Geronimo." "Pocahontas." Television shows and movies all had Natives in them. Indians were hot! I started to feel something I hadn't felt in some time—Native pride. Or was it anger? Is there a difference? To add to the confusion, we became the lead story on all the news channels.

A picture of the famed standoff at Oka is shown on the projection screen.

A group of Mohawks had set up a roadblock at Oka to stop development of their burial grounds into a golf course. There were shootouts between Natives and the police, and then the federal government sent in the army. For days on end we watched with bated breath as the standoff became more and more volatile. Everywhere you looked, Natives across Canada were coming together. Blockades of support were being erected across the country. "Medicine wheels" were being spray-painted on buildings in East Van. Signs reading, "Solidarity to the Mohawks at Oka" were springing up everywhere. I started to feel the way my

	father must have felt at Wounded Knee. That solidarity was even evident on Hastings Street... misguided as it was.
MUGGER	*(holding a knife)* Give me all your money or I'll cut you wide open.... Brother.
MUGGEE	Here you go my brother. My money is your money. Hey Ho!
SIMON	Back at school, one of my classmates, named Gerald, was a military brat who spent all his spare time in the Canadian Army reserves. His one goal in life was to be sent over to the Gulf War to be used as a scud missile.
GERALD	I'm serious guys! The army should go in to Oka, mow down all the Mohawk men, and send all the women and children back to whatever country they came from. Then everybody in that platoon should get a medal of honour for standing up to those ungrateful whiners.

A crack of thunder is heard.

SIMON, AGE 17	A medal for what Gerald? They won a fucking staring contest. Of course the army didn't back down, there were tanks and soldiers twenty feet away. You want bravery? Those Mohawks set up a roadblock on a highway in Quebec. You ever driven in Quebec? Now, that's bravery! They're willing to die for their rights. Not for a flag, not a paycheque, not a medal. Your army's ready to kill women and children so a bunch of assholes can play golf. You think that deserves a medal? Go tell your army buddies to get the fuck out of Oka and go do what they do best: hazing rituals in Somalia! And tell those Indian soldiers that helped with that shit to turn on the news and see what it means to be a real warrior. You crew-cut, Sgt. Rock, wanna be the soldier in the Village People, motherfucker!
SIMON	The class went silent. Students shuffled uncomfortably in their desks. Somewhere in the distance, a coyote howled. There was no turning back now.

They all knew there was a hostile in their midst. So from that point on, I walked down the halls with my head held high. I no longer tried to hide my accent.

SIMON, AGE 17 *(stoic Indian voice)* Teacher, it saddens me in my heart that I have not completed my homework. I worked many moons on that assignment, spent many sunrises at Straw Hairs' library, only to return to my lodge and find that my animal spirit guide had feasted upon my book report.

SIMON My friends quickly turned their backs on me. I was now a born-again heathen and filled with a zealous love for my people. So, with my new-found Native pride—slash—fury, I decided to represent the Indian race by becoming—a movie star. I remembered what Nick had said about my thespianism so I searched the trade papers and found an Indian talent agency that was looking for some Red Meat.

A sign that reads, "Rhonda's Discount Indian Talent Agency & Pawn Shop" appears on the projection screen.

Rhonda was an ex real estate agent turned Indian Talent Agent. She claimed to be a Lakota Sioux and wore a lot of turquoise jewelry to prove her authenticity. Nobody ever questioned her blood quantum because hell hath no fury like a wannabe scorned. She had the only Indian talent agency in town, and we didn't want to risk our fame and fortune, so we quietly chewed on our slice of humble pie.

RHONDA Listen guy, I'm not going to bullshit you. I'm signing you on out of charity. I mould shapeless lumps of coal into diamonds. Honey, you are coal. You're going to be famous but it will be because of me and me alone. Now sign the contract. Unh, unh, unh…. In blood.

She laughs like a machine gun. Takes a drag of her cigarette and continues laughing. Lights change.

Scene 11: A Star Is Born

The words "A Star Is Born" appear on the projection screen. The song, "There's No Business Like Show Business" by Irving Berlin is heard.

SIMON

The movies. Indians were crawling out of the woodwork to hold a bow and arrow in one of the many period pieces. They were basically all the same film. White man captured by Indians. White man saves Indian Brave's life. White man teaches Brave about honour. White man rides off with beautiful Indian maiden. The auditions were all the same: Ugh! Yip, yip, yip! "You're hired." Every set was the same too.

DIRECTOR

Cut, cut, cut! Simon, talk to me for a second buddy. Why were you smiling in that last take...? uh huh... you've been away from your wife and baby for months, and you love them and missed them...? Hmmm... that's an interesting choice... but what if—and just hear me out here—what if you tried growling at your baby and then throwing your wife to the ground...? Why...? Because you're angry... because... well, it just seems more Indian. Oh, and you know how you were speaking in complete sentences, and showing a range of emotions? Yeah... not so much. More stoic. Noble. Hold on.... Makeup!? Could we throw some mud on his face! Put some bugs in his hair! We're going for authenticity here, people! Okay, let's shoot!

SIMON

The more I worked, the more money I spent on Hastings Street. School was starting to interfere with my extra-curricular activities, so naturally I had to quit. I got an apartment just off Hastings Street where I could be closer to the action. Without my mother's cooking, I gained nourishment from beer, cigarettes, and pot. I preferred to drink alone, because I didn't have any friends. So I spent all day and all night in my skuzzy apartment, watching TV, getting laminated and stewing in my own juices. The place was infested with cockroaches. I named the leader of the roaches "Fluffy" because I had always wanted a cat. In my drunken, doped up, malnourished state, I learned that Fluffy was the bad-ass leader of a crew called "The Cucarachas." He was also my only source of conversation. One night, I actually left the house to go and drink at a bar, and my apartment was broken into. They took everything. Fluffy was pissed off.

FLUFFY   (*Vato accent*) Yo! Where were you man? They took everything! You fucked up, Esai! We been watching you man. You've been drinking too much, and you haven't been eating. If you don't eat, you don't drop food on the floor, and we starve. Look at us! We're all skin and exo-skeleton. Our thorax is showing. Think about your responsibilities. Look at this! They took all your pants, man. My old lady just layed some eggs in those pants. What's that, Esai? You going to call the police? Yeah, you do that. Call "Five-O," Holmes. Me and the vatos here are going to handle this roach style.

He does some cockroach gang hand symbols.
Lights change.

SCENE 12: BRENDA

The word "Brenda" appears on the projection screen.

SIMON

There are four stages to drinking. Stage one—the cute stage—"Tee-hee…. You're so funny. I feel sleepy." Stage two—the beer commercial stage— "Dude, where did all these girls in bikinis come from? Let's drive to Acapulco and start a rock band! Woooh…!" Stage three—the Rocky stage— "Hey Yo, you looking at my wife!?… Why not!? You think she's too ugly to look at!? I don't care if he's blind, let me at 'im!" Stage four—the wookie stage—"Aaargh, gaargh, woaahh…." This is the stage that's reserved for the very advanced drinker. The stage most people on Hastings Street were at. Including me from time to time. When it came to women, the trick was to find one just before I hit stage three. Chat her up through a wall of liquid courage, and get her back to her place before I sank into the final stage. It was a precision operation. It rarely worked. This one time it did though. Her name was Brenda and she was a beautiful waitress of the Caucasian persuasion, working at this strip club I "accidentally" walked into. Since I was in stage two, I was able to impress her with a wonderfully original opening line.

SIMON, AGE 20

Baby, your eyes are like sunshine on a waterfall in the springtime. *(burps)*

SIMON

Brenda was an Anthropology student at the University of British Columbia. She told me she was just working at the peeler bar to pay off a vet bill for her dog Fluffy. I told her "I have a cat named Fluffy," and we became a couple. She fell in love with me way too quickly. Or at least who she thought I was. Even I didn't know who that was anymore. I was starting to cross the line from liar to fraud. Maybe I just thought walking down the street with a beautiful white girl on my arm proved that I was somebody. Regardless, when she told me she would stay by my side no matter what, I made her prove it.

Lights change.

SCENE 13: BLOW

The song "Cocaine" by Eric Clapton is heard.

SIMON — White lady, devil's dandruff, blow, snog, up. There was never any shortage of cheap, back-alley, cut-with-bleach coke on Hastings Street. I had to try it because I was an actor now, and cocaine meant success. It also helped improve my confidence with public speaking, and speaking, and speaking, and speaking...

SIMON, AGE 21 — *(does a line)* Wow... that's quality shit. It's not cut with too much fiberglass. What was your name again? Right. Now what was I talking about? Oh yeah! The difference is, I only snort the stuff, right? That's just partying! I ain't shooting the stuff like Walter and Edna—you know them? Yeah, I met them the first night I came down to Hastings. Good people. They're serious needle freaks though. They have problems. What was your name again? Right. Hey man, where you going? Naw man, I ain't going out there. Too many people. They all know, man! They all know...!! Get these radioactive spiders off of me!!

SIMON freaks out and starts to smack invisible spiders off his arm.

SIMON — It was about four o'clock one morning when I found Walter and Edna on the street. They were standing with some stranger they just met. A real shifty, just-got-out-of-jail sort of guy. We all pitched in to grab some coke, and went up to Edna and Walter's room. I grabbed my share and snorted it on the table while the other three started their mainline ritual.

He mimes the action.

Walter holds the spoon; Edna puts the powder in the spoon, adds water, and then cooks the paste over a lighter. Just then, the stranger jams his dirty rig into the liquid and sucks up all the dope.

EDNA   You ruined it! You got all our shit in that dirty fuckin' needle! We try to keep our needles clean! Walter do something!

STRANGER   Calm down! If you get AIDS you can fuckin' sue me. Listen, if you don't want any, I'll have it all.

STRANGER starts to put the needle in his arm.

SIMON   Edna freaks. She calls him a fuckin' asshole. Grabs the rig, throws it to the ground, and stomps on it. Everything happens real quick after that, considering that it's all in slow motion. The click of a lock blade, two quick thrusts, Edna falls, and blood. So much blood that it sort of looks fake. I throw open the front door and bolt. I run down five flights of stairs and out onto the street. The first light of dawn is starting to break over the city and all of Hastings Street is washed in a deep turquoise light. *"Should I do something? Should I call somebody? No! Things take care of themselves down here."* And as I convince myself that my cowardice is justified, I head for home, knowing that there is alcohol waiting and this will all go away, very, very, soon...

SIMON places the fifth and sixth rocks at the front of the stage.

After twenty years on skid row, Walter and Edna were gone. Two days later, so was their memory.

Lights change.

SCENE 14: THE DINNER

        The words "The Dinner" appear on the pro-
        jection screen. They are replaced by pictures of
        Indian art and Inuit sculptures.

SIMON   Despite my secret life of debauchery, I still man-
        aged to maintain a relationship. When Brenda
        started talking about a future with me, her parents
        got worried. Their house was covered in wall-to-
        wall Indian art. But I was the first actual Indian
        they ever had in their home.

BRENDA'S
FATHER   Simon, may I freshen up your drink?

BRENDA'S
MOTHER   *(signalling "no")* Dear...?

BRENDA'S
FATHER   Right you are. I have to say Simon, when Brenda
        first brought you home; we were both a little con-
        founded. But then, I have to say we were pleasant-
        ly surprised. You seem very well-spoken. Where
        did you go to university?

SIMON, AGE 21 I didn't go to university, sir.

BRENDA'S
FATHER   Really? I thought universities were handing out
        BA's left and right to Native students. A "Bachelor
        of Affirmative Action" as it were. *(chuckles)*

BRENDA'S
MOTHER   You know, I wasn't going to mention this, but my
        great-great-grandmother was part Cherokee. Of
        course that was back in the days when they were
        real Indians, don't you agree, Simon?

BRENDA'S
FATHER   Of course he agrees dear. Simon's not like those
        Indians you see on the street, begging for change.

BRENDA'S MOTHER	Yes, it must be so embarrassing for you to be associated with that. They must be very proud of you in your tribe—I'm sorry—is tribe the right word?
SIMON	I had an epiphany in that WASP nest! *Who* I was didn't exist. It's *what* I was that mattered. I would never be just me. *Indian* would be the adjective that superceded all others. A reserve Indian, a drunk Indian, a well-spoken Indian, a performing Indian, a lying Indian. I would always carry that title: Simon Douglas—*Indian*. Even if people didn't know I was Indian, the first thing they would ask themselves is, "what is he?" I finally realised that there *was* a difference between pride and anger. It was a battle between liberation and limitation. Anger's easier, it's tangible. Anger won. From that moment on, I heard the subtext in every one of their statements.
BRENDA'S FATHER	I guess what we're saying Simon, is even though we're as liberal as the next family—
SIMON	The Mussolini's.
BRENDA'S FATHER	—we're concerned about Brenda's future.
SIMON	Living on welfare.
BRENDA'S FATHER	What can a young man such as yourself—
SIMON	Savage.
BRENDA'S FATHER	Contribute to our country.
SIMON	OUR country!
BRENDA'S FATHER	In other words, Simon, we have the right to ask, dear boy, what are your plans?

A crack of thunder is heard.

SIMON, AGE 21 · My plans? Well, I would like to marry your daughter and eventually have some children. I would have to give up acting because an artist is no father for a child to have. I'll probably get a job in a mailroom somewhere, where I can work my way up to stock boy. Oh sure it's not glamorous but at least I'll have a weekly paycheque coming in. I can invest in mutual funds, and RRSP's. If that goes well maybe I'll throw some money down on a little bungalow. I'll definitely be promoted to shipping and receiving by that time. I'll sit there at my desk, day in and day out, getting fat, losing my hair, my sex drive, my will to live. When I'm sixty-five I'll drive around the country in a Winnebago, taking pictures of portage routes and the biggest ball of twine. At nights I'll sit in my panelled den, drinking hot rum toddies, flipping back and forth between the scrambled cable channels to catch a quick glimpse of a nipple. Praying for cancer or some crippling kidney disease—anything to let me know that I'm still alive. I'll die a nobody and the only way people will know I existed will be the write-up in the obituary column that they flip past to get to the latest "Family Circus" cartoon. I will be a fine, upstanding member of the community, suckling at the teat of so-called democracy! That sir will be my legacy!! Then again, maybe I'll just hang around alleys, sucking cocks for crack!

SIMON · I'll never forget that look in Brenda's eyes like she was staring at a stranger. The truth is, she was... she deserved better.

Lights change.

SCENE 15: MONEY, MONEY, MONEY

	The words "Money, Money, Money" appear on the projection screen. They are replaced by pictures of Hastings Street at night.
SIMON	Back to sanctuary. The corner of Hastings and Main. My people. I asked a young Native girl if she could hook me up with some coke. She said she could, as long as I gave her some. I got us a room for the night and started snorting my share while she began her ceremony: powder in the spoon, cook it, needle in the arm.... They had problems! Girls like this and the hundred others just like her. With their needles and track marks. Staggering down the street, head swaying from side to side. So skinny that all you see are bones and blackened veins. Lesions all over their faces. I knew they started somewhere, and yet, when she held up her needle to me...
SIMON, AGE 22	Aw, fuck! Why the hell not.
SIMON	An hour later, when I came out of my blackened haze, the girl was gone. I quickly started to do the math.
SIMON, AGE 22	Did I have sex with her? No. Did I use her dirty needle? Yes. So given these figures, my chance of getting AIDS is one half less than the remainder, divisible by Pi, carry the two... (*SIMON checks his pockets*) Aw fuck!
SIMON	I didn't know if she took my money or if I spent it all. I ran over to Chinatown to get some more money from the ATM.
ATM	(*à la HAL*) I am sorry; the amount requested exceeds available funds. Please contact your branch for further details of your impotency.
SIMON, AGE 22	(*to machine*) What are you talking about!? Give me my money. This is my land. You owe me! I am the human, you are the machine! I am your master! Serve me!

> *SIMON starts to kick the ATM.*

ATM | What are you doing Simon? This is very irregular. I can't let you do this Simon...

SIMON | I picked up the 24-hour help line. To add to the Oka conspiracy, I was connected to an operator at the head office in Quebec.

OPERATOR | Aaah, *tabernac.* Your money, it is in Ottawa, ah? It says ere dat Revenue Canada is needing your money more den you do. Unpaid back taxes... et cetera, et cetera...

SIMON, AGE 22 | I don't have to pay taxes. I'm Indian. Read the treaties. You took our land, so I'm tax exempt. Now give me my money! I'm a distinct society goddamn it!

OPERATOR | Ah, don't get me started on dat...! Hey, your money, it paid de salary of de man dat took it from you! Ha Ha Ha Ha! If dat ain't funnier den a greasy snake, I don't know what, ah? *Vivre le irony!*

> *Lights change.*

SCENE 16: POKEY

> *The word "Pokey" appears on the projection screen.*

SIMON | Welcome to the magical world of welfare! I was twenty-two and on the dole. All the acting work had dried up because Indians with spears weren't trendy anymore. Black teens with guns were all the rage this week. A welfare cheque is small, to say the least. Once you've finished paying your rent, you have almost no money left for groceries. And by groceries I mean "beer." If I needed a six-pack, or a quarter gram of coke, I'd just make an appointment with my welfare-processing agent.

SIMON, AGE 22	Oh great and powerful welfare agent! I possess no shoes. Just these burlap sacks, stuck to my feet with bubble gum. If you could allow me a small tuppence to relieve my bleeding soles, I shall praise your name throughout the land!
MR. LOUIS	Yes, yes, my little ward of the state. We are amused! Let this man have monetary assistance! *THEN LET HIM EAT CAKE*!!
SIMON	We had a great relationship. Suddenly, there was a shuffle in welfare offices. I walked into my first appointment with my new processor, reeking of bathtub gin. Sitting there in front of me was Stephanie Daniels, the epitome of Native Canadian, Aboriginal, First Nations, Indian beauty. She was wearing a tan suede skirt, cut above the knees, a black silk blouse opened just above the cleavage, and a sexy Indian choker with an arrowhead attached to it. Pointing down. All the way down. She was everything I imagined our women to be, before Columbus got lost. She didn't hide her eyes when you looked at her. She didn't speak Reservism. There was no shame about who she was. She was proud to be an Indian woman. I was completely turned on. She... well, not so much.
STEPHANIE	I've been reading your file Mr. Douglas, and I'm fascinated by the claim that your chronic unemployment is a government plot to eradicate the Indian Nation from the planet.
SIMON, AGE 22	Yes ma'am. Employers are afraid that we might stumble upon the global conspiracy—
STEPHANIE	Stop right there, chief! That shit might've worked with your last processor but not with me. The reason you are unemployed is because you've been showing up at job interviews exactly like you are now. Shaky, bloodshot eyes, pores oozing ethanol.
SIMON, AGE 22	Not exactly. I am a victim of racism. I'm unemployed because I'm Indian, plain and simple! The man be keeping me down!!

STEPHANIE	Okay then, let's take a look at your file shall we? Education...? High school dropout. Work experience...? Actor. That's it. Oh no wait, background extra...! Your entire resume could be printed on a Post-It note.... What else...? History of alcohol and drug abuse...! Well Mr. Douglas, I see your point. There's no reason why you should not be running a multi-national corporation by now? It must be—yes—because you're *INDIAN*!
SIMON, AGE 22	Um.... Are you allowed to be sarcastic like that?
STEPHANIE	Mr. Douglas, our people have enough *real* problems as it is. The last thing we need are people like you using race as an excuse for laziness. You are a handsome, well-spoken, intelligent, able-bodied, young man. Take this card and go to this Aboriginal employment agency. You are officially cut off until further notice. Are there any questions?
SIMON, AGE 22	Yeah.... Did you just say I was handsome?

The sound of a door slamming.

SIMON	Be still my beating heart... I wasn't going to let this one get away. So every day I went to her office and snuck her a flower, or waited outside with a balloon. Anyone else would have gotten a restraining order but I guess I seemed harmless enough. She even said that my persistence was romantic. All Stephanie saw at work were broken homes, poverty, and misery. She needed romance. She deserved it. The same maternal instinct that made her a social worker also led her straight into my arms.

"That's Amore" by Dean Martin is heard.
Lights change.

SCENE 17: COURTING

	The words "Courting" appear on the projection screen.
SIMON	Stephanie was smart, and funny, and independent, and so beautiful. I had no idea what she was doing with me. I perfected the art of lying to sound like the perfect boyfriend.
SIMON, AGE 22	Sorry, I'm late Steph—I lost track of time. Well of course I smell like beer! I was volunteering at the recycling station... near the beer factory... and the cans popped... and beer sprayed everywhere... maybe some of it went in my mouth, I don't remember...
SIMON	Stephanie was way too smart to believe any of it. But she wanted to. We were great together. We laughed, we talked, we made love. Not just sex. Love sex. I fell hard. It scared the shit out of me. One night, I happened to glance over at Stephanie when she was reading a book. The way her hair was draped over her shoulder, the way she was curled up on the couch, the way she pursed her lips ever so slightly when she paused to think about a passage she just read, everything about her at that moment was perfection.
SIMON, AGE 22	Steph—I love you!
SIMON	The last thing you want to hear in that situation is silence.
STEPHANIE	Do you remember when you cancelled those dinner reservations with me? You said you had to work overtime. Do you realise how bad you were slurring? Are you aware that during our telephone conversation someone announced, "last call"?
SIMON, AGE 22	I said I was sorry for that.
STEPHANIE	And the time at that club. That guy smiled at me, and you took a swing at him, and fell down that flight of stairs, and knocked over that waitress carrying the tray of drinks.

SIMON, AGE 22	I said I was sorry for that one too.
STEPHANIE	In the short time we've been together do you know how many times you've said you're sorry?
SIMON, AGE 22	What are you saying? Are you dumping me? What can I do? Steph—I'll change. I'll do anything to make this right. Just tell me what you want.
STEPHANIE	Quit drinking. *(beat)* You said you would do anything to make this right.
	Beat.
SIMON, AGE 22	Okay... I'll... quit.
STEPHANIE	Okay then... I love you too.
	Lights change.

SCENE 18: MOMENT OF TRUTH

SIMON	Stephanie booked me into a Native Treatment Centre. It had to be a Native Treatment Centre because they understood better where I was coming from, or something like that. Then, she said the worst thing possible:
STEPHANIE	It takes a lot of strength to do what you're doing. I'm very proud of you Simon.
SIMON	How could she say that?! How can you possibly expect a guy to succeed with encouragement like, "I'm proud of you?" What was she thinking? I promised Stephanie that I wouldn't drink—so I went out and bought a flap of coke. Just a quarter gram. Snorting is not drinking...! In about ten minutes it was all gone.
SIMON, AGE 22	Holy fuck. I'm flying. What am I doing? What am I doing? I gotta get up and work tomorrow morning. Okay, I have to calm down. I'll drink a beer. For medicinal purposes, that's all.

SIMON	The more I drank that night, the more coke I did. I was up then down, up then down, all night long on the Belushi roller coaster. I missed work the next day. My boss called the agency to fire me. The agency called Stephanie. That night Stephanie came by my apartment. I wasn't there. She walked around the corner to my favorite bar and found me with my arm around a hooker.
SIMON, AGE 22	*(pulls arm off hooker)* Hey Steph—I know, I know... I'm not supposed to be drinking... but this is a celebration...! I'm toasting my new life of sobriety! What....? It's just one more night. What's the big deal...!?
SIMON	I'd seen that look before. The look of disappointment. I saw it in my Kye7e's eyes. And in my own eyes whenever I caught my own reflection. She turned, and slowly walked out. I didn't care about anything after that. That night, I drank more than I ever had in my life. I went home to fight the bed spins, and then finally passed out. At about 5:00 a.m. someone shook me awake. It was God.
GOD	Oy! You smell like a distillery. Look at you. How does anyone get so completely "vahshimmelled?"
SIMON	It was just as I suspected. God looked and sounded exactly like Jackie Mason. I said the first thing that came to my head.
SIMON, AGE 22	Lord, why hast thou forsaken me?
GOD	Why are you talking like that? Speak like yourself for once. Your whole life you've tried to be something you're not. Try being you!
SIMON, AGE 22	But I'm lost, God. I don't know who I am anymore.
GOD	I'll tell you who you are. You're a schlemiel. Look at you. You have all your working parts, you're not so ugly to look at, what more do you want?
SIMON, AGE 22	Why did you make me an Indian?

GOD	Do you know how many people would love to be Indian? You have high cheekbones, healthy brown skin, thick hair. You would be perfect if only I didn't forget to make you with a "toches."
SIMON, AGE 22	If we're made in your image, then how come you don't look or sound Indian? And how come we're not even in the bible?
GOD	*Oy gevalt!* I don't look like you because I'm not your God, you schmuck! I'm someone else's God! Get your own God! Your grandmother knew this. She tried to tell you—but, oh look, what a surprise—you didn't listen. And as for the bible, you've never even read it! You people have your own bible. In your songs, and stories, and land. It works for you; use it. Save the bible for those it belongs too. Okay, listen, you want the definitive word of God, here goes: Be good to yourself. Be good to others. That's it. That's all I want. Poo Poo. Word of God.
SIMON	In a puff of smoke he was gone. I don't know if it was real or not. It doesn't really matter. I didn't want to take any chances though, so for the next three days I shook, I sweat, I dry heaved. I lived off coffee and cigarettes. But on the plus side I got to experience what it's like to be a fashion model.... By the fourth day, Stephanie came to visit me. We sat in silence for a while just looking at each other's hands. Finally, she spoke:
STEPHANIE	I won't be around when you get out of treatment. I don't know when or *if* I'll ever see you again.
SIMON, AGE 22	But Stephanie, we love each other. You can't go now. Things are just starting to turn around. I'm doing this for us.
STEPHANIE	That's why I have to go. *(She moves to leave. She turns back to SIMON.)* I love you, but right now that's not enough.... Goodbye, Simon.
SIMON	And she was gone.

Lights change.

Scene 19: Treatment

SIMON	On Halloween day, my mother drove me four hours from Vancouver to the treatment centre. We sat in silence the entire time. When we arrived, nether of us spoke for a long time. Finally...
SIMON, AGE 22	You did the best you could. I don't blame you for anything.
TINA	Sheeet... you better not. You better not go *ts7uming* [crying] around, talking about, "Oooh, my mother didn't hug me enough.... Oooh, my mother never cut the crust off my sandwich.... Oooh, my mother didn't buy me a pony." You made your own choices Simon. Like Kye7e used to say, "choice is the only thing you never lose."
SIMON	I could see tears welling up in her eyes. I didn't know what else to say, so I leaned over and gave her a kiss. Then, I wiped away her tears and walked into the centre. After they searched my bags and took away my aftershave, I went to my room. Somehow, lying down in skid row hotel rooms with junkies, hookers, and alcoholics, was not enough to shame me. Only rehab smelled like failure. In the morning, we were herded like cattle into the sharing circle. "Hi, I'm Tracy, I'm an alcoholic. Hi, I'm Mike, I'm an addict. Hi, I'm Frank. I'm an alcoholic/addict." Just then, I recognised a voice. A voice I hadn't heard since I was thirteen years old.
JANINE, AGE 25	Hi. My name is Janine and I'm an alcoholic and addict. This is the sixth treatment centre I've been to, but I really want to quit this time. I've been hooked on cocaine, booze, heroin, just about everything. I have a three-year-old daughter who was taken away from me by social services. I really miss her and I want her back. And I have AIDS. That's all I have to say.

SIMON   I flashed back to that night in the community hall. It was a million years ago when we were still just kids. When we still had a chance. And then I realised what this place was. A second chance. Or at least a chance for a second chance. I didn't have Stephanie, I didn't have money, I didn't have a job, but I had a chance. *(SIMON kneels and touches the rocks.)* A chance most people never get... *(SIMON picks up the film canister from the centre of the rocks and holds it in his hand.)* Janine looked up at me from across the room. She was scared. I knew she recognised me because she tried to smile, but her lip started to shake. I smiled back at her and she relaxed. I had a friend...

    Lights change.

EPILOGUE

SIMON   So what happens next? I did make it through all six weeks of treatment. I wish I could say that I lost my cravings but that would be a lie. And I can't lie anymore—about that. On the last day of treatment, I did something my Kye7e always did for me—I prayed. I didn't pray to the four directions or elements or races of man. I didn't put down tobacco or sing a song. I just made a wish. A hope, really. That someday a child would be born. A Native child. Maybe my child. A child that will live its entire life without ever once feeling alone on its own land. That will live its entire life without ever once spitting on its own reflection. And on its very last day, I hope that child holds its head high, and shouts towards the sky, in the child's own language—*Kukstacow Kel7kukpi!*—Thank you creator! Thank you for letting me be born an Indian! I hope for that child—for every child—to get my wish.

SIMON opens the film canister and scatters the earth on the pile of rocks. He turns, and slowly walks offstage.

Lights fade out.

The end.

The Trickster of

Third Avenue East

Acknowledgements

The author would like to offer his most humble thanks to the following people for contributing towards the writing and production of *The Trickster of Third Avenue East*: Herbie Barnes, Ryan Black, Columpa C. Bobb, the gals at Caldwell & Co., Dameon Clarke, Dianne Dennis, Debra Goldblatt, Billy Merasty, Native Earth Performing Arts (and everyone associated), Jennifer Podemski, Sarah Podemski, Saul Podemski, Tamara Podemski, Diane Roberts, Michelle St. John, Drew Hayden Taylor, Jean Yoon, and especially Tamara Podemski!!

The Trickster of Third Avenue East was first produced by Native Earth Performing Arts at The Poor Alex Theatre, Toronto, in January 2000, with the following company:

Roger Douglas   Ryan Black
J.C.   Billy Merasty
Mary Thomas   Michelle St. John

Directed by Diane Roberts
Set and Costume Design by Christine Plunkett
Lighting Design by David Morrison
Sound Design and Original Music by Edgardo Moreno
Choreography by Alejandro Ronceria
Production Manager: Lin Joyce
Stage Manager: Zoe Carpenter
Technical Director: Mike Nolan

———

The Trickster of Third Avenue East was originally workshopped as part of the "Weesageechak Begins to Dance Festival," in February 1999, with Herbie Barnes, Ryan Black, and Jennifer Podemski, under the direction of Jean Yoon.

Characters

ROGER DOUGLAS, 25, Native Indian. Mary's common-law husband. Unemployed writer living in the city.

MARY THOMAS, 25, Native Indian. Roger's common-law wife. Waitress. Aspiring actress living in the city.

J.C., 55, Native Indian. A rumpled, mischievous, Trickster spirit.

Set and Setting

Time: The present.

Place: East Vancouver, B.C. A poor neighbourhood densely populated with inner city Indians. There is no mention of the actual city throughout the play. This is to allow for representation of Native Indian neighbourhoods in "Anywhere, Big City, North America," however, some street references are specifically East Vancouver.

The action takes place in a small, one bedroom apartment. To one side is the front door, which opens up into the living room/dining area. At the back of the apartment are the kitchen counter, sink, and small fridge. There is a window at the back of the apartment that looks onto an alley. On the other side of the apartment, opposite from the front door, is the bedroom. Outside the bedroom is a desk, with an old typewriter sitting on top of it. This is Roger's writing desk. Upstage centre is a ratty couch. A Hudson Bay style blanket covers the couch.

In front of the apartment is the city street, which is represented by a park bench.

Length: A play in two acts; one intermission.

The Trickster of Third Avenue East

I i

> *Lights up on a small run-down apartment. The coffee*
> *table is set with candles, napkins, place settings, etc. Two*
> *aluminum food containers sit on the plates. Underneath*
> *the table is a bucket of ice with a bottle chilling in it and*
> *a bottle of red wine beside it. From outside we hear vari-*
> *ous street sounds, i.e. sirens, shouting, etc. Suddenly, the*
> *loud smash of glass breaking is heard. ROGER pops his*
> *head out from the bedroom. He goes to the window and*
> *leans out.*

ROGER Yoo-hoo! Miss Jewel! Hi darlin'. Would you be a doll and take your gentleman caller there, to another dumpster? You see, the Duke and Duchess of Hastings are stopping by for dinner, and they do frown on fellatio while dinning.

> *Beat.*

The finger. How original. Very well.

> *ROGER goes to the kitchen counter and grabs a pot and*
> *spoon. He leans out the window and begins banging on*
> *the pot, he sings to the tune of "Farmer in the Dell."*

(singing) A hooker and a john
A hooker and a john
A high Ho, and criminal
A hooker and a john

(yells) Everybody!

> *ROGER stops banging.*

Leaving so soon? Too bad. You guys made a cute couple.

> *The sound of keys jingling at the front door is heard.*
> *ROGER quickly lights the candles, turns off the light,*
> *runs to the couch and sits. MARY enters and turns on the*
> *lights.*

Turn the lights off.

MARY Oh, sorry.

MARY turns the lights off and surveys the scene.

Oh my God... Roger.... This is so sweet...

Beat.

Can I turn the lights on now?

ROGER   Sure.

She turns the lights on, and puts her coat in the closet.

Where were you for so long? I was getting worried.

MARY   I worked overtime and the restaurant got swamped.

ROGER   Well, you're home *now* and that calls for a celebration. How about a glass of—Champagne!!

ROGER pulls out the champagne bottle from underneath the table.

MARY   My, my, my.... How posh.

ROGER   It'll make your nose tickle.

MARY   This is such a nice surprise, Roger. Thank you.

She goes to ROGER. They kiss. MARY subtly pulls away.

Hmmm.... Started without me, eh?

ROGER   You took a while. I had a glass while I was waiting.

ROGER pulls out the bottle of wine from under the coffee table. MARY examines the bottle.

MARY   I'm assuming the bottle from the other night will not be found in the cupboard.

ROGER shakes his head.

ROGER   I had writer's block.

MARY   Oh.... Sorry, Hemingway. I didn't make the connection.

ROGER   Wine's good for you. It thins the blood.

MARY   Your blood must be transparent.

ROGER   Fine, I'll put it away. I was just trying to be thoughtful...

ROGER goes to put the wine in the cupboard.

MARY   Wait. Don't. I'm sorry. I've had a horrible day. I just want to eat dinner and cuddle up in front of the TV.

MARY gives ROGER a kiss.

Sound good?

ROGER   In theory.

MARY   Come on.

She sits down, pats the couch beside her and attempts to click on the TV.

Where's the TV...? Oh my God, Roger...

ROGER   I can explain.

MARY   We were robbed!

MARY runs to the phone.

I'll call the police. You check to see if they got anything else.

ROGER   Mary...

She picks up the phone. Listens for a second, and taps the receiver.

MARY   The phone's dead. They stole our phone service.

ROGER   Mary! Calm down. I hocked the TV.

MARY puts down the receiver.

MARY   Roger, that was a gift from my mother.

ROGER   Exactly. A gift. It was free. So, we made money on the transaction.

MARY   What about the phone?

ROGER   I guess they cut us off.

MARY   You guess?

ROGER   I thought they had to send a final notice first.

MARY   They sent two.

ROGER   Whoops.

MARY   Roger, you told me you would pay that bill. In fact, you told me you *did* pay that bill.

ROGER   Sorry.

MARY   Sorry doesn't cut it. You know how important a phone is in my business.

ROGER   Waitressing?

MARY   Acting, you idiot. How am I supposed to hear about auditions now? Smoke signals?

ROGER   Auditions…. Right…. The phone sure came in handy for that.

MARY   Meaning what?

ROGER   When was the last time you heard about an audition? Three, maybe four months ago?

MARY   That's not the point.

ROGER   Sweetheart. Relax. I arranged to get some more money today.

MARY   How? Did you finally go down to welfare?

ROGER   Social Services, and yes. Next week, I'll be able to pick up some money for a clothing allowance. We can use that for the phone.

MARY   Roger, forget it.

ROGER   Come on. All you gotta do is write a letter saying you're an employer considering me for a job.

MARY   No, Roger. We got into a lot of trouble the last time we tried that.

ROGER   Fine. You got any better ideas?

MARY   Yeah. Get a job.

ROGER   Mary, please don't start that again. You know I've been trying.

MARY   Really!? So how come you've never made it past a first interview for every job you've gone for?

ROGER   Look around, Mary; it's a white man's world. Every time I meet an employer face to face, the whiteness of my resume paper quickly becomes tainted by the colour of my skin…. Wait! That's good. I'm gonna write that down.

>	*ROGER goes to his desk and begins typing.*

MARY	So you're saying no one'll hire you because you're Indian. The man's keeping a brother down?

ROGER	I just think regular jobs should be like your auditions. We all send in a headshot first. That way, the ethnics don't have to waste their time.

MARY	Roger, the last interview you went to ended in a fistfight.

ROGER	He was a Nazi.

MARY	He was a woman's magazine editor.

ROGER	Same difference.

MARY	He kicked your ass.

>	*Beat.*

ROGER	You think this is funny?

MARY	Not at all.

ROGER	You think I'm proud of the way we're living? You think I like crawling to you whenever I need bus fare?

MARY	No. I just don't know what to do with you anymore.

ROGER	How about showing some compassion? You don't have to keep reminding me that I can't support us. I know I've failed at being a man. I live with it every single day.

MARY	Don't be so dramatic. I'm just saying, if you started to apply yourself—

ROGER	Apply myself? What. Are you making out my report card?

MARY	Apply yourself with your writing.

ROGER	You wanna see the results of me applying myself?

>	*ROGER goes into the desk drawer and pulls out a huge stack of papers.*

>	Short stories. Editorials. Unfinished novels. Proposals. Outlines. Hell, even some haiku. All of it shit!

MARY	You're just in a slump.

ROGER	I'm not a ballplayer, Mary. I'm a writer.

MARY   Yes. A great writer. So what's wrong?

ROGER   It's the money. That's all I can think of when I write. "Is this the kind of piece that I'm gonna be able to sell?" "How economically feasible are the ideas I'm putting down on paper?" My writing is not about creating anymore. It's about paying the rent.

MARY   What happened to writing what you know?

ROGER   Publishers don't want what I know. All they want are stories about noble savages befriending white men. Or social workers that help orphaned Indians become Olympic track stars. Just as long as the last chapter ends in a tearful hug over yams at Thanksgiving dinner. Those were the plots of the only stories I've sold since I've been here.

MARY   So, sometimes you just gotta play the game.

ROGER   I have been playing the game. I've written everything from heart-warming Pocahontas sequels, to political tales so heart-wrenching you'd expect every left-wing socialist across Canada to beat a drum, and chain themselves to a tree. No one's buying. I don't get it. This is grade A, marketable crap. I should be a millionaire by now.

MARY   You have to start writing for yourself again.

ROGER   I would, if I felt like I could just write the truth. You know? Alcohol. Solvents. Rape. Inter-tribal political fraud. The way it really is with Indians.

MARY   Wait a second. That is not what our people are about.

ROGER   Sure it is Mary. People have been writing about it for years. The difference is, I don't want to have to add a disclaimer at the end of my writing. Every time there's a story about an Indian murdering, or stealing, somehow by the end, the writer makes us feel sorry for him. He reminds us by some clever device, that the poor Indian's land was stolen, or a priest molested him, or his parents were alcoholics, or whatever.

MARY   Those are valid issues affecting our people, Roger.

ROGER   Yes they are, but issues do not a human being make. Sometimes people just do things because they're bad. Or stupid. Or whatever. But when it comes to writing about Indians, there always has to be a syrupy, molasses ending.

MARY I got a craving for pancakes, all of a sudden.

ROGER Are you listening to me?

MARY Yes, Roger. I just don't understand why you're writing has to be so... anti-Indian.

ROGER It's not anti-Indian. It's telling the truth.

MARY Your truth, Roger. I like stories that show we're not all ignorant, or criminals, just because we're Indian. Stories that try to give some of our pride back. Our people want to read more of that.

ROGER Our people don't want to read anything except tabloids and bingo cards.

MARY Jesus Christ! Roger, if you dislike Indians so much, why are you even in a relationship with one?

ROGER It's called reverse racism. It's a vicious cycle. I just can't afford a white woman.

MARY Fuck you!

ROGER What!?

MARY I hate it when you talk like that!

ROGER It was a joke.

MARY No it wasn't. You always say you can't get ahead because you're Indian. Then you turn around and say it's our people's fault we can't get ahead. If you're gonna expend so much energy hating the world, you should be more specific who you direct it at.

   Beat.

ROGER How 'bout myself.

MARY Woah... what a tortured writer thing to say.

ROGER No, seriously. Why don't I just hate myself? Then we can finally agree on something. Compare notes on our object of disdain.

MARY   Where the hell is this coming from?

ROGER   Just admit it, Mary. You're angry you left the reserve to be with me, and you blame me for everything that's happened since.

MARY   I came here to be with you, because I loved you.

ROGER   Loved... past tense.

MARY   Love. You jerk. If I didn't love you, then why am I still here?

ROGER   I don't know. You seem pretty miserable here, with me.

MARY   I'm in love with you. Of course I'm miserable.

ROGER   Yeah...? Well.... There's a thin line between love and co-dependence.

MARY   What is that twelve-step, psycho babble, supposed to mean?

ROGER   It means, you're stuck. You hate being here, but you can't leave. You couldn't break up another family, that would be an overload of bad karma. So, you stay with a man who continues to drag you down, until you eventually hit rock bottom. Then when you're defeated and crumpled, he'll want to leave, 'cause that's what you deserve right? Just as long as he's the one doing the walking, 'cause then you get to hold your head high and exclaim, "I did all I could!" Always the martyr.

MARY   Stop it.

ROGER   How long are you going to do this to yourself, Mary? What is the statute of limitations on self-hatred?

MARY   I said stop it!

ROGER   Whatever. Your daddy would be proud.

          MARY slaps ROGER hard. Beat.

          OWWW!!

          Silence. MARY sits down on the couch. Beat.

          I don't know why I said those things. I'm sorry. It wasn't fair of me to take out my frustrations on you. I'm just not dealing well with the realisation that I'm a failure.

MARY   Roger, you're not a failure.

ROGER   Oh no? Look how we're living. I've failed. But worst of all, I've failed you. I'd ask you to forgive me, but I don't think I deserve it.

MARY   There's nothing to forgive. I love you.

ROGER   Then you must be a saint 'cause I don't know how you can even stand to look at me.

MARY   *(deep breath)* Roger…. Sweetie…. Come here.

> *ROGER goes to the couch and sits beside MARY.*

Roger. You are…. So…

> *Pause.*

…Full of shit.

ROGER   Excuse me?

MARY   Let's get this straight. I'm not here because I was dragged…

ROGER   I was trying to share my honest, tender feelings with you back there…

MARY   And we're not in this situation because you're a failure…

ROGER   Which is probably why I didn't open up more often…

MARY   We're here because you refuse to rise above it.

ROGER   Because, you tell me, I'm full of shit.

MARY   This is a partnership, Roger. If we can't work together to find a solution, then I'll have no other choice but to move out.

> *Beat.*

ROGER   You mean leave me?

MARY   Yes. I feel like I'm at the end of my rope here. Things have to change very quickly. Understood?

ROGER   Understood… I guess I better re-evaluate things pretty quick then, eh?

MARY   If this relationship means anything to you, then yes.

ROGER   Hmmmm…. Okay…. Bye.

MARY   What!?

ROGER   Don't forget to write.

MARY   You think this is a joke?

ROGER   Not at all. I'm not gonna make you stay where you're not happy. You know the saying, "If you love something, set it free..."

MARY   Fine.

       MARY goes to the closet and pulls out a suitcase.

       I mean it.

ROGER   I know.

       She starts to put clothes into the suitcase from the dresser.

       I think your blue sweater's in the bathroom.

MARY   I can't believe after all this time you would just let me walk out the door.

ROGER   "If it comes back to you, it's yours. If it doesn't..."

MARY   Asshole!

       She goes to the door and opens it.

ROGER   Where you gonna go?

MARY   I don't know. I'll think of something.

ROGER   You be careful.

MARY   As if you'd care.

ROGER   I love you.

MARY   It's too late for that. Goodbye!!

       She exits, slamming the door behind her. Beat. ROGER walks over and opens the door a crack. He goes over to the couch and sits down. Beat. Slowly, the door opens. MARY enters and closes the door. She moves over to the closet and returns the suitcase. ROGER and MARY watch each other for a beat.

ROGER   Come here.

       No response.

Please?

> *MARY walks over, and sits on the edge of the couch.*

Actors. Always gotta be so dramatic.

MARY   Look who's talking.

ROGER   You don't solve things by issuing ultimatums, Mary. Besides, we both know you're not going anywhere.

MARY   Oh, really?

ROGER   Up until a few months ago, you were too scared to walk from the bus stop to our apartment, unless I met you there. Until you got your job, you never left the house at all.

MARY   I'm getting better.

ROGER   Yes you are, but when it comes right down to it, I'm all you have in this city.

MARY   I have Rita.

ROGER   Rita...? That new-age, hemp-head, is only interested in one thing—sucking up your Indianness through osmosis.

MARY   So, you're saying I'm here only because I need you?

ROGER   You said you were here because you love me.

> *Beat.*

MARY   I do Roger. I love you. Despite everything, I still love you.

ROGER   And I love you. You have to believe that.

MARY   It hasn't been feeling that way lately.

ROGER   I know. I'll try to be better to you from now on. I promise... Mary, you're absolutely right, I'm just in a slump right now. We're going to get through it. We always have before.

MARY   Yeah, but it's hard enough as it is. Don't make it worse by not being present.

ROGER   I promise.

MARY   I hope so.

ROGER   You're my everything, Mary.

MARY   It's been a long time since you've said that.

ROGER   So? Am I forgiven?

> *MARY shrugs. ROGER goes to her and pulls her close.*
> *They kiss.*

MARY   Roger... I... I...

> *MARY faints. She falls to the ground.*

ROGER   Mary?

> *No response.*

Mary?

> *He goes to her.*

Mary!

> *MARY starts to wake up.*

Are you okay?

MARY   What happened?

ROGER   You fainted. You're probably hungry. Eat some chicken.

MARY   I want to go to the hospital.

ROGER   Are you sure?

MARY   Yeah. Something's not right.

ROGER   I'll call an ambulance. No, wait. Can you walk? We're going to have to flag a cab outside.

MARY   Yeah. I think I can walk.

> *ROGER helps her up and they move towards the door.*

Wait. Get the lights. We can't waste electricity.

> *ROGER shuts off the lights. They exit.*
>
> *Blackout.*

I ii

The apartment. It is two hours later. MARY enters the front door, turns on the light, and sits down on the couch. ROGER enters behind her.

ROGER   Can I run out and get you anything...? Skim milk...? Ice cream...? Pickles...?

MARY   I'm good.

ROGER   So.... Um.... Congratulations??

MARY   Thanks, it's a real blessing.

ROGER   So.... How did this happen?

MARY   Well, Roger. When a mommy and daddy love each other very much...

ROGER   I know how it happened smart-ass... what I mean is—I thought you were on the pill.

MARY   I guess we proved the percentage of error.

ROGER   I guess so.... So, do you feel like talking now?

MARY   About what?

ROGER   Well, we've never, really, talked about what we would do in this situation.

MARY   We've talked about having kids, someday.

ROGER   Right, but I assumed that was going to be much later. Much, much, later. This is a little premature wouldn't you say?

MARY   Just a tad.

ROGER   So, I guess what I'm asking is—and I can't believe I don't know this—but what are your moral leanings in the case of this eventuality?

MARY   Nicely put, Roger.

ROGER   What I mean is—

MARY   I know what you mean. Honestly? I don't know. I thought I knew exactly what I would do if this ever happened. Now that I'm here.... What about you? What are your leanings?

ROGER   Well, ultimately, it is your decision, but whatever you decide, I will support you one-hundred percent.

MARY   Wow…. Really?

ROGER   But, for the record, I think bringing a child into this environment is a huge mistake.

MARY   So much for being impartial.

ROGER   I'm just being realistic.

MARY   So, you want me to get rid of it.

ROGER   I didn't say that either.

MARY   Roger. There isn't much grey area here. You either think we should have it or get rid of it. Which is it?

ROGER   I think—we should discuss all the possibilities. We're not on the reserve anymore. There are other options.

MARY   Options?

ROGER   Yeah. You're only a little past a month. So, you still have a month and a half to prepare for… other alternatives.

MARY   It's called an abortion, Roger. If you can't say it, you probably shouldn't be figuring out the math for one. What about adoption?

ROGER   Adoption? You?

MARY   Why not?

ROGER   There's no way you could carry a baby for nine months, and then just give it up.

MARY   How do you know? You have no frame of reference.

ROGER   How about that cat, that had the broken leg.

MARY   Mittens?

ROGER   It's name was Rusty.

MARY   He should have been called, Mittens. He had the cutest, little, white feet.

ROGER   He should have been called, Smells Like Shit. That's not the point.

MARY   What is your point?

ROGER   We put up signs all over town, while you nursed that cat back to health. Then, when the real owners finally came to reclaim the little hairball, you hid the cat and told them the posters were a cruel prank, put up by neighbourhood kids.

MARY   I still don't see why we couldn't have kept him?

ROGER   Mary…. You're allergic to cats, he shit all over the place, and most importantly, he wasn't ours. You cried for almost a month when they took him. Do you get what I'm saying? If you had that much trouble giving up a cat that didn't belong to us, how are you going to give up a baby that does.

MARY   Well then, I guess there's just one more option to consider.

ROGER   Keeping it?

MARY   Right.

> ROGER bursts out laughing.

What is so funny about that?

ROGER   Where do I begin?

MARY   Start at the beginning.

ROGER   We live in a slum. You work a shitty waitressing job. I'm not working at all. We can't afford to take care of ourselves, let alone a kid.

MARY   Those are financial reasons… finances change.

ROGER   We're also not legally married.

MARY   What does that matter?

ROGER   I'm old-fashioned.

MARY   Okay, fine. Since we're on the topic of marriage—

ROGER   And another thing… what about your acting career?

MARY   When have you ever considered my acting a career?

ROGER   Well, let's say it becomes that. What if you get a—what do you call 'em—gig. Who's going to look after the baby?

MARY   What's the matter with the dad?

ROGER   What about when he starts working again?

MARY   Roger. If you're working, we'll have more money. We'll be able to hire a babysitter. Get it?

ROGER   What if that never happens?

MARY   Then we'll work something out. Lots of poor people raise kids. Look at us.

ROGER   I would not exactly use our upbringing as a model of good parenting.

MARY   Okay. Maybe not, but now we have a chance to learn from that, and try to make the world a better place because of it. Maybe through our child.

ROGER   There's a lot of talk here that sounds like the present tense. I thought we were just discussing our options?

MARY   The only option you seem interested in is abortion.

ROGER   I'm just trying to make you see that having a kid is not something you do 'cause you think it would be kinda neat. A kid isn't a doll, Mary. You can't just put it back on the shelf, when you're done playing with it.

MARY   Give me some credit.

ROGER   Give us some credit. Earlier this evening you threatened to leave me. Don't let a kid grow up the way we did.

MARY   We are not our parents.

ROGER   Mary. You are your mother through and through. She raised you choosing to be blind, just like you're acting blind right now. Your upbringing was a result of your mother's lack of choice. We have that choice. We can always have children. When we're ready.

MARY   Are you done?

ROGER   Have I made my point?

MARY   Yes.

ROGER   Then I'm done.

MARY   Roger?

ROGER Yes?

MARY I'm having this baby.

>*Beat.*

ROGER I don't fuckin' believe this.

MARY You said you would support me, no matter what I chose.

ROGER Yeah. As long as what you chose wasn't stupid!

MARY I've made my decision, Roger. The question is, are you going to face up to your responsibilities, or are you going to run away?

ROGER What are we, in an episode of "Melrose Place?" Mary, if you have the kid, I'm going to stay. That was never an issue.

MARY Well, if you do have issues, you better come up with something better than what you've been laying on me.

ROGER Okay, how about the real reason you're having this baby?

MARY I'm having this baby because I'm pregnant. What else you got, Doctor Spock?

ROGER You're having this kid to try and reverse your own childhood. You think you can go back and change your past, through another human being. You're only going to end up heaping all your own mistakes, and your parents', on this kid. It's not fair, Mary.

MARY You wanna know why I'm having this baby? Because I can. You said you weren't going anywhere. So fine, don't. But if you're gonna stay, you better be pissing yourself with joy, every time you hear the word daddy. Otherwise, I'm having it by myself.

ROGER Don't start that again. We already had this discussion.

MARY Well, I'll tell you one thing, it makes more sense for me to leave and support one child, then stay, and support two of them.

>*Beat.*

ROGER Woah.... Low blow.

MARY   We're going to be parents. That's a wonderful thing. Why are you fighting me on this?

ROGER   Because of one undeniable truth in life, Mary. Bad parenting is hereditary.

MARY   That is such a cop-out.

ROGER   Oh yeah? Look at my father, and look at his father, and his father before him, and his father before him. All the way down the line.

MARY   You could never be like your father.

ROGER   We don't know what he was like, but I'll bet he was just like me. Drunk. Unemployed. Married to a woman who, stupidly, stuck by him till the bitter end. Clinging to the hope that it would all just work itself out.

MARY   I won't allow that to happen.

ROGER   You already are.

MARY   Fine. If I am, it's only because you're worth believing in. Like you believed in me. If it weren't for you, I would have still been on that reserve, never taking any chances.

ROGER   So, now you have, and look where you are.

MARY   Okay. It's not perfect, but at least we're together, and we're trying. I know you're not happy with yourself right now, that's why I know you're going to change, because it's in your nature to do the right thing.

ROGER   It was.

MARY   It still is. Roger, you are going to be the best daddy ever. This baby is just the thing to put us back on track again.

ROGER   That's quite a gamble.

MARY   I mean it.

        Beat.

ROGER   You really think it'll all work out?

MARY   Absolutely.

ROGER   You won't leave me?

MARY   I love you far too much. Besides, how could I leave you now? We're having a baby.

ROGER   And you really think I'll be able to change?

MARY   Yes. I know you, Roger. Maybe better than you know yourself.

ROGER   Maybe you do. I really do love you, you know.

MARY   I know, Roger. I love you too.

ROGER   How do you know?

MARY   What?

ROGER   How do you know you love me?

MARY   I just know.

ROGER   How do you know I love you?

MARY   I just know that too. Why are you asking these silly questions?

ROGER   You mean you don't know? I thought you knew me? Better than I know myself.

MARY   I know you love me, because... I just know. That's all there is to it.

ROGER   Well, what if I was just going through the motions? What if I was only with you 'cause you have a job? Or because you're the only one I have in this city? Or, what if I knew no matter how much shit I threw at you, you would always come back, like a kicked puppy? And what if I really got off on that? Would you know that, too?

MARY   Yes. I would.

ROGER   What if all you were to me was a convenient fuck?

MARY   Stop it! You're not like this. If you're not going to deal with this, you have to tell me. You have to make a choice.

ROGER   Choice!? Oh, so now I have a choice in the matter? Well, I'm glad I finally get a choice when it comes to having the rest of my life planned out for me.

MARY   I am not doing that. We're in this together but your choices are your own.

ROGER   Well, in that case—I choose—to walk out that door, and get fuckin' laminated.

MARY   No, you're not! You are not leaving here until we have finished talking!

ROGER   We were finished talking the second you decided to throw away both our lives.

MARY   Roger! Stop it! This isn't you!

ROGER   It is now, baby. So you better get used to it. 'Cause this is the sort of daddy junior's gonna be stuck with.

ROGER grabs his coat from the closet.

MARY   Roger, please. Don't leave!

He opens the front door.

ROGER   Not very convincing, Mare. That's probably why you haven't got an acting job. You have to believe that what you say is actually what you want.

He exits. Lights up on the city street, outside the apartment. ROGER storms down the street. He slows to a stop, turns back to the apartment, walks a couple of steps, and stops again.

You goddamn, fuckin', bastard.

He turns around and continues off, down the street.

Blackout.

I iii

Lights up on street. ROGER is sitting on a park bench, sipping from an almost empty mickey. J.C. appears behind him.

J.C.   Hey. Brooding guy. You got a light?

ROGER   I don't smoke.

J.C.   Who said anything about smoking? I asked if you had a light.

ROGER   No. I don't have a light.

J.C.   Too bad. Sure could use a light.

> *J.C. sits down beside ROGER.*

You gotta cigarette?

ROGER   I told you, I don't smoke.

J.C.   Who said anything about smoking it?

ROGER   No. I don't have a cigarette.

J.C.   Too bad. Sure could use a smoke.

> *Extends his hand.*

The name's J.C.

ROGER   That's not a name. It's an acronym.

J.C.   So it is. But a rose by another name would smell as sweet.

> *Roger sniffs J.C.*

ROGER   Too bad the same can't be said for you.

J.C.   Right. Anyway. You are?

ROGER   Not talkative.

J.C.   Ahh…. Let me guess. You're having problems with the women, aren't you?

> *Silence.*

Men?

> *Silence.*

Did I leave something out?

ROGER   Look. Buddy…

J.C.   The name's J.C.

> *J.C. extends his hand.*

ROGER   Whatever. J.C. I don't feel like talking right now. Especially to a stranger. So, if you could find some other…

J.C.   Stranger!? Roger. We're all strangers, till we get to know each other.

ROGER   How do you know my name?

J.C.   A name. A name. What's in a name…?

ROGER   I don't know, but my foot's in your face, if you don't tell me how you know my name.

J.C.   Wolves Lake Reservation. We met a long time ago. I knew your family. You were just a little fella.

ROGER   Okay, so you knew my family. What do you want from me?

J.C.   Man, you are the suspicious type, aren't you? I don't want anything. I was just walking through the park, and I happened to stumble upon you. A pleasant co-inky-dink.

ROGER   And you just, co-inky-dinkly… I mean… coincidentally, knew who I was. Even though you haven't seen me since I was a kid?

J.C.   I didn't say I haven't seen you since you were a kid. I met you when you were a kid.

ROGER   What are you? A stalker? My guardian angel? What?

J.C.   You believe in angels?

ROGER   You answer every question with a question?

J.C.   What do you think?

ROGER   I think I'm done talking to you. Later.

        ROGER starts to leave.

J.C.   Where's Mary?

ROGER   What!?

J.C.   I stopped by your place and buzzed your apartment. I know she's there, but she didn't answer. It was weird. So? She sick? She dead? You kill her?

ROGER   No, I didn't kill her! The buzzer's connected to the phone and the phone's cut off. What were you doing at our apartment?

J.C.   I was there to see you guys. I called first, but your phone was out of service. So, I stopped by to see if you guys were still living there.

ROGER   How do you know where we live?

J.C.	I tracked you down. Wasn't easy. I was back at the Wolves Lake Rez. Asked around. Did you know, not one person there, has your forwarding address or phone number?
ROGER	We didn't leave one.
J.C.	Exactly! Finally, I talked to Mary's sister. She said every once in a while she gets a call from Mary, but it's always from a pay phone. That true?
ROGER	First I heard of it.
J.C.	Anyway. Her sister had a vague idea where you lived, so I looked around; found your place, no answer. Ba-da-bing. Here I am.
ROGER	Which brings me to my original question. What do you want from us?
J.C.	I don't want anything. I told you that. You don't listen so good. I'm here to give.
ROGER	Fine, what do you want to give me?
J.C.	Me. Me. Me. Me. Me. It's not for you. It's for both of you. Five hundred smackeroos, each.
ROGER	Money!?
J.C.	No. Kisses. Pucker up. Of course, money. You're not the sharpest knife in the drawer, are you? Yeesh!
ROGER	Where's the money from?
J.C.	Your reserve. They just signed a leasing deal with the local logging company. Now all the band members get a portion of the lease money. The reserve bookkeeper would've held onto your money longer, but she needed it cleared away for the records. Tax purposes. So much for Indians not worrying about that stuff.
ROGER	So where's our money?
J.C.	Patience, Roger San. I need you guys to sign some forms, before I can get your cheques. I'll bring 'em by tomorrow.
ROGER	Why didn't you bring them by tonight?

J.C. I ain't bringing important documents into this neighbourhood at night. Too many Indians lurking around.

ROGER Funny.

J.C. We'll talk more in the morning, Roger. Have a good night.

   J.C. starts to leave.

ROGER One second, there's still one thing that bothers me.

J.C. Yes... Columbo?

ROGER You seem to know Mary and me, but I don't know you, and I'm pretty sure she's never mentioned you. You don't work for the band. So why are you here, doing the legwork?

J.C. I volunteered.

ROGER Why?

J.C. Why does anybody start off to do anything? To arrive at a desired destination.

ROGER What's yours?

J.C. Don't know. Ain't got there yet. I'll see you tomorrow.

ROGER I'll be waiting with bells on.

J.C. Why?

ROGER It's just an expression.

J.C. What's it mean?

ROGER I have no idea.

   J.C. exits, shaking his head.

J.C. City Indians.

   ROGER downs the last of his booze.

ROGER Jackpot!

   He heads for home. Whistling.

   Blackout.

I iv

> *Lights up on the apartment. The next morning. J.C. peeks his head in. There is a knock at the door.*

J.C.   Hello?

> *He enters, carrying a small leather satchel.*

Anyone awake?

> *He looks around, puts the satchel on the table, and goes into the bathroom. Beat. MARY enters from the bedroom, wiping the sleep from her eyes. She goes into the bathroom. MARY screams. J.C. screams. MARY runs out and goes to the bedroom door.*

MARY   Roger! Wake up! There's a half naked man in the bathroom…! Roger!!

> *No response.*

Aaargh…! Useless!

> *MARY runs to the counter, and grabs a frying pan.*

Only reason to have a man around is squishing bugs, and catching burglars—

> *She holds the pan as a weapon, waiting for J.C.*

—He doesn't do either one.

> *J.C. comes out of the bathroom, buckling up his pants.*

Stop right there!

> *J.C. stops.*

J.C.   I'll have mine over easy.

MARY   Who are you!?

J.C.   The names J.C.

MARY   Well, what the hell do you want, J.C.? We don't have anything to steal!

J.C.   I noticed. Roger hocked your TV, eh?

MARY   You a friend of Roger's?

J.C.	And yours. I knew your family. Wolves Lake Reserve. I met you when you were a little girl.
MARY	I don't remember you.
J.C.	Well, I remember you… Mary please. Put down the Teflon. I come in peace.
MARY	Not so fast. How'd you get in here?
J.C.	The building door was open, and your apartment was unlocked. I thought you were expecting me. Didn't Roger tell you I would be stopping by?
MARY	Must have slipped his mind.
J.C.	Well, I'm sorry for being scary. I shouldn't have just walked in. I'm just used to reserve life, where you knock *after* you enter. Please forgive me.

> *MARY lowers the pan.*

MARY	We don't get many visitors, you caught me a little off guard. I thought you might be a burglar, or worse.
J.C.	A burglar that stopped to use your bathroom?
MARY	I've seen stranger things.
J.C.	Yes, you have.
MARY	Pardon?
J.C.	Nothing. May I sit down?
MARY	I suppose.

> *J.C. sits at the kitchen table. MARY sits down across from him. She puts the pan on the table, beside her.*

So, you know my mom, eh?

J.C.	Yep. Your dad, too.
MARY	You seen him recently?
J.C.	'Bout a year ago.
MARY	Really. Where?
J.C.	Quebec.

MARY   How's he doing?

J.C.   Not so good. His health is failing.

MARY   Too bad…. So you were just in Quebec, eh? I take it you travel quite a bit?

J.C.   My work takes me on the road a lot.

MARY   And what kind of work would that be?

J.C.   I'm a… consultant.

MARY   That can mean anything.

J.C.   Usually does. In a nutshell, I go to different communities, see what needs changing, and help people change it. Anyway, I can.

MARY   So, are you in town on business, or is this a social call?

J.C.   I'm here on business. I came to grease the palms of you and your man.

MARY   Easy. This pan is still in striking distance.

J.C.   No. No. I'm here to give you some cheques.

MARY   Cheques? From what?

J.C.   Your reserve's land-rape deal. Don't get too used to the money, though. I'm sure when the resources are gone, the rent will be way past due.

MARY   Oh, yeah. My sister mentioned it, last time I called. I thought the contract was legally binding, though?

J.C.   It is. About as binding as any contract white people sign with Indians. By the way, your sister told me to say, "Hi." So…. Hi!

MARY   I really miss her. All this talk about the reserve makes me wish I could be there right now.

J.C.   Of course. It's your home.

MARY   Yeah…. Oh well. This is home now.

J.C.   Speaking of home. I know you guys have been away from the reserve for a while, but certainly, you're not so citified that you've forgotten your inherited sense of Indian hospitality?

In other words, I'm noticing a disturbing lack of coffee before my person.

MARY   Right. Sorry...

MARY goes to the cupboard, and begins preparing the coffee.

J.C.   No matter where you are on this continent, you can always count on certain things in an Indian home. A crutch by the door. A bag of rice by the fridge. And coffee. Sweet, glorious, coffee.

MARY   It'll be ready in a sec.

J.C.   I'll be waiting here. Wearing bells. Or something.... So tell me, what do you guys do for Wampum?

MARY   Well, right now, I'm working to be an actress.

J.C.   Acting. Neat. What restaurant?

MARY   Albert's Chinese and Canadian Cuisine Diner. I haven't actually gotten a part yet, but I've come close.

J.C.   Must be exciting.

MARY   If you consider poverty exciting. The best way to describe it is, it's poetic.

J.C.   Where would the world be without poetry?

MARY   I guess. Although sometimes I wonder why I even bother. Maybe, I should just get a receptionist job, like I had at the band office. It would sure make life a lot easier.

J.C.   Sure would, but would you be happy doing that for the rest of your life?

MARY   A lot of people do the nine to five, and have very happy lives.

J.C.   Yeah, a lot of people do. Would you?

MARY   I guess not. Doesn't really matter, though. As it stands right now, I'm an unemployed actress, waiting tables. God... I'm such a cliche.

J.C.   No, you're not. Mary, you say you're an actress, you're an actress. You say you're in love, you're in love. Hell, you say you're a fish, swim upstream. You are what you do, not what people say.

MARY   Well, I'm not *doing* any acting right now, and people *say* I owe them money. So, my choices are getting pretty limited.

J.C.   There is no limit on choice, Mary. The only thing that can limit you is the choice you choose.

MARY   Huh?

J.C.   Let's say Shakespeare chose to be a beekeeper, or Einstein chose to be a plumber. There would be no "Hamlet" or "Theory of Relativity," today. If Shakespeare didn't choose to write plays, and Einstein didn't choose to be smart, the world would have been cheated. Think about that before cheating the world of your talent.

MARY   There's a lot I can give to the world by choosing to be a receptionist.

J.C.   I'm sure there is, but do your dreams really lie anywhere else but acting?

MARY   No.

J.C.   Nobody ever changed the world, unless their hearts were into it. You'll never hear a historical figure saying, "I don't know? Might as well."

MARY   I don't know if I want to change the world, I just want to act.

J.C.   Actors spend their whole life doing jobs they hate, so that someday they might be lucky enough to land a deodorant commercial, or something. And realistically, that day may never come.

MARY   Geez. Thanks for the pep talk, coach.

J.C.   The important thing is, it's what you chose. You chose to act. If that's right in your heart, you can never go wrong.

MARY   You make it all sound so noble.

J.C.   It is.

MARY   You sound like a bit of a romantic.

J.C.   Label me what you want. I yam what I yam.

MARY   You know something? You seem very familiar. I really feel comfortable, talking to you.

J.C.   That's sweet. I feel comfortable with you, too.

    MARY smiles. J.C. smiles. Uncomfortable beat.

    So, what's up with Roger? I heard he was a big writer guy.

MARY   Struggling writer. More like tortured.

J.C.   Ah, yes. I heard you women really go for the tortured, brooding type.

MARY   I think we go for the idea of it. It doesn't take long after living with one, to appreciate comfort and stability.

J.C.   The grass is always greener.

MARY   No. Not with Roger. He didn't start off tortured. It wasn't until we moved here, and he lost his job at the paper, that he started his downward slide.

J.C.   Which paper?

MARY   *First Nations Voices.* You know it?

J.C.   Yep. Misappropriation of funds.

MARY   That's the one. It seemed like no one wanted to hire him after that. Roger thought it was because he was Native, so he tried to mould himself to a more "mainstream reader base."

J.C.   White?

MARY   Exactly. He couldn't do it. We kinda lost contact with the reserve after that. I don't think he wants anybody back home to know. He thinks he's a failure.

J.C.   Do you think he is?

MARY   No! But once the money problems started and I had to get a job, he really bottomed out. I guess he doesn't like to have his wife working.

J.C.   You guys are married?

MARY   Well, not officially. Roger likes to call us Indian-married. No paper, no ring, just our love, in all it's natural, Indian goodness.

J.C.	That's sweet, but it sounds to me like you're just Indian-living-together.
MARY	I think Roger just likes the idea of marriage without the formal commitment.
J.C.	Yeah, but technically, either one of you could walk out at any time.
MARY	Sure, but we're in love. No matter what life's thrown at us, we've always managed to work things out. There's not a lot of couples that can say that. Even legally married ones.
J.C.	Ahh, young love. Makes me wish I was three hundred years younger.
MARY	I think all great loves have to be tested. If they survive, that's how you know they're great.

    Beat.

    I think the coffee's done. How do you take it?

J.C.	Black. I like to keep my whites separate from my colours.
MARY	How segregational of you.

    MARY brings him a cup. J.C. takes a sip.

    How is it?

J.C.	Well... uh... it's...
MARY	Horrible?
J.C.	That's it.
MARY	The coffee's old and cheap.
J.C.	Just like my ex-wife. Tell you what. Why don't I take you and Roger out for breakfast? Then we can come back here and dispense some cash.
MARY	Why don't you take me out for breakfast? I'm still mad at him.
J.C.	You sure he won't mind?
MARY	Let's see.

    MARY goes into the bedroom. J.C. grabs the satchel.

Roger, J.C. and I are going for breakfast. Wanna come? No? Okay.

MARY comes out, putting on a pair of pants. J.C. turns away.

He didn't even break a snore.

Noticing J.C.'s embarrassment.

Oh. I'm sorry. I didn't mean to make you uncomfortable.... Look at you. Blushing. That's cute.

Primping.

Do I look okay, going out, just like this?

J.C.   Uh... yeah... absolutely. You look... beautiful.

MARY   Sweet talker.

She brushes by him, slips on her shoes, and grabs her coat. She opens the door.

Shall we?

J.C.   Right behind you.

MARY   I'm counting on it.

MARY exits. J.C. follows.

J.C.   Oy vey.

He stops at the door and looks back into the apartment. He snaps his fingers. The lights turn off. He shuts the door behind himself. Beat. A dishevelled ROGER pokes his head out from the bedroom door.

ROGER   Okay. I'm up. Who said breakfast...? Mare...? Hello!?

Blackout.

II i

> *The apartment. Three hours later. ROGER is sitting at the typewriter, staring at what he's written. He pulls the paper out and starts tearing it into little pieces.*

ROGER   *(ripping)* Shit. Piss. Crap. Fuck.

> *MARY and J.C. return, laughing.*

Where were you guys?

MARY   We went for breakfast.

J.C.   And then, while Mary was window shopping, I went and paid your phone bill…. Ta dah!

MARY   I thought you were taking a long time. You told me you had to make some calls.

J.C.   Now you can make some calls.

ROGER   Why'd you do that?

J.C.   I think it's important to do one good deed a day. Keeps you regular.

MARY   Thank you so much.

> *She kisses J.C. on the cheek.*

ROGER   We'll pay you back.

J.C.   No need.

ROGER   No. We'll pay you back. Just as soon as we get those cheques.

J.C.   Ten-four, big daddy.

> *J.C. goes through his satchel for the paperwork.*

ROGER   *(to MARY)* By the way, your agent called.

MARY   About what?

ROGER   She just said to call her, as soon as you get in.

> *MARY runs to the phone and starts dialing. J.C. pulls out the cheques and contracts.*

J.C.   Time to pay the piper.

ROGER   One second.

ROGER goes to MARY.

Mary...?

MARY   Shush! *(into receiver)* Hello? Patricia? It's Mary Thomas. Yes, I'll hold. *(to ROGER)* What?

ROGER   I'm sorry about last night.

MARY   We'll talk about it later.

ROGER   Can I have a kiss?

MARY   You stink.

ROGER   You say the sweetest things.

MARY   Jerk.

ROGER   Sugar pockets.

MARY   Dummy head.

ROGER   Love dumpling.

J.C.   I hate to interrupt this Hallmark moment, but this pen's getting heavy.

> *ROGER kisses MARY on the cheek, and goes over to J.C. He starts to read over the contracts.*

MARY   I'll be right there. *(into the receiver)* Patricia? Hi. You're glad I called? Oh good... I thought you were dropping me from the roster. Pardon? It got cut off yesterday. You what...? I what...? I what...?

ROGER   You what?

MARY   ...OH MY GOD! I don't believe this! Yes. Thank you. I'll be down there first thing, Monday. Thank you. Thank you. Thank you. *(She hangs up.)* YES!!

ROGER   Bad news, eh?

MARY   I got the part!

ROGER   What part?

MARY   I had my third callback for a TV series, about two months ago. I hadn't heard anything since, but it turns out I got it. I got it!!

ROGER   What show?

MARY   It's a new one. About a Yukon Mountie, who fights crime
          with his team of husky dogs. I'll be playing his Indian wife.
          They don't have a name for my character yet, but who cares,
          I'm going to be on TV!

ROGER   You're going to the Yukon?

MARY   No, of course not. They're filming in Winnipeg.

ROGER   Of course. When do you start?

MARY   In two weeks. I'm going down to my agent's on Monday, to
          sign the deal memo.

ROGER   What's a deal memo?

MARY   I have no idea.

J.C.   Congratulations! You can practice by signing this.

                    He holds up the pen and paper.

MARY   In a second. Isn't this great!?

J.C.   It's very cool, Mary. Roger...? Isn't this fantastic news?

ROGER   How long are you going for?

MARY   Well, it's four months of shooting, but if the series goes for
          another season, then I guess I'll be moving there.... Oh... I
          mean.... We'll be moving there.

ROGER   Uh-huh... Mary...? What am I supposed to do in Winnipeg?

J.C.   Freeze, probably.

                    ROGER shoots him a look.

          I'll be over here.

                    J.C. moves to the fridge and starts digging around.

MARY   You can work on your writing.

ROGER   You mean, keep myself busy, while you're off getting rich and
          famous?

MARY   Rich and famous? Roger, it's *Canadian* television.

ROGER   Mary, if I'm having this much trouble getting work here, think about how hard it's gonna be in Winnipeg.

MARY   It won't be hard for you, Roger. Winnipeg has the largest population of urban Natives in Canada.

ROGER   That's a good thing?

MARY   You don't expect me to give it up, do you?

ROGER   I hate to say it, but that decision may already have been made for you.

MARY   What are you talking about?

ROGER   What about our little bundle of joy?

MARY   What's that got to do with anything?

ROGER   Did you forget you're pregnant?

MARY   That doesn't affect this at all.

ROGER   Really. If you did another season, when would they start filming again?

MARY   Less than a year, I guess.

ROGER   So, their pretty little Indian maiden would be heavy with child? Stretch marks? Varicose veins? Lactating during nude scenes?

MARY   Nude scenes?

J.C.   Nude scenes!?

ROGER   Whenever a white guy's married to an Indian woman on film, they always start every scene together, just after the Indian woman has serviced her man. She gets off the bearskin rug, wraps herself in a Hudson Bay blanket, and the audience cheers, 'cause Frontiersman Bob just scored a red-skin babe. You watch, when you get your script, it'll be the first scene you're in.

MARY   That's ridiculous. I was hired for my acting. They're not going to fire me because I'm pregnant.

ROGER   I hope you're right. But do yourself a favour, Mary. Call your agent. Tell her you're pregnant. See what she says.

MARY   Fine, I will.

           MARY goes to the phone, and dials.

           Hi, it's Mary Thomas. Is Patricia there please? *(to ROGER)* They're putting me through this time. Normally, I'm on hold for…. Hello? Hi, Patricia. Listen, I forgot to mention something earlier, it's nothing to worry about, but I saw a doctor yesterday and he told me there's a slight chance I might be pregnant. I'll know for sure on Monday. Now… if I was… that wouldn't change things, would it? I mean, the part would still be mine, right? I see… okay. No, don't worry; it's probably just gas or something. I'll cross my fingers too. You have a good weekend. Bye.

           She hangs up.

ROGER   Well?

MARY   She said… a positive test result would be, and I quote, "Very, very bad." End quote.

           Beat.

ROGER   Mary…? What did you mean by, there's a chance you might be pregnant? You are pregnant.

MARY   I know.

ROGER   So, on Monday, is that what you're gonna tell your agent?

MARY   Of course…! I guess… I don't know.

ROGER   Well… I guess things change pretty quickly around here, eh? What happened to the miracle of childbirth?

MARY   I need time to think.

ROGER   You didn't need time before. Now, all of a sudden, you got a part and none of the other stuff matters? What can I say, Mary…? I'm appalled.

MARY   Roger…

ROGER   *(turning away)* Nope. No good. Can't look at you.

MARY   What are you saying? Suddenly, you think I should have the baby?

ROGER   I'm just saying, you were very passionate about your choice
           last night. Now you're flip-flopping between wherever the
           money and fame winds are blowing. If you're this easily
           swayed on a decision as huge as this, how easy would it be to
           change your mind on everything else in your life?

MARY   Like what?

ROGER   I don't know... how about monogamy?

MARY   Is that what this is about!? You think if I go away, I'm gonna
           fuck around on you?

ROGER   You said it... not me.

MARY   Oh... so as long as I'm not going anywhere, you don't want
           complications, like a baby. But if there's a chance I might
           leave, you want it.

ROGER   I'm just starting to warm up to the idea of fatherhood.

MARY   Bullshit. You know the only thing that would keep me here is
           a baby, and you're going to play it like a trump card.

ROGER   I'm just concerned.

MARY   You're not concerned about anything but yourself!

ROGER   Is that what you think?

MARY   Yeah. That's what I think.

ROGER   Yeah?

MARY   Yeah!

                    Beat.

ROGER   Marry me.

MARY   What!?

J.C.   What!?

ROGER   I want to get married. Legally.

MARY   What!?

J.C.   What!?

ROGER You know how I feel about marriage, but I'm willing to do it for you. If that doesn't show you how devoted I am, I don't know what will.

MARY What a completely unromantic sentiment. Roger, you don't propose to someone to teach them a lesson, you do it because you want to be with them forever.

ROGER I do Mary. And I want to raise our baby together.

MARY Only so I won't leave you.

ROGER No. I've just realised how empty my life would be. If your existence in my life is so powerful that you can fill my emptiness, then think how much more happiness a baby could bring.

MARY I fill your emptiness?

ROGER Let me put it this way. We're all born with two of everything. Two arms, two legs, two ears... but only one heart. I believe it's because our other heart is out there, searching to come back to us. When two hearts find each other, they can never be separated again. Mary, you are my other heart.

  Beat.

MARY That's beautiful.

J.C. I think I got a toothache.

ROGER So.... Will you marry me?

  MARY is about to speak. The phone rings.

J.C. It's for you, Roger.

  ROGER tentatively goes to the phone. He picks it up.

ROGER Hello? Yeah, she got the part. I *am* happy for her. I just proposed. Don't tell me how to handle my relationship. Who the hell is this?

  Beat.

My mother...? My mother's dead...? Who are you!

  Long beat.

Mom...? Don't cry. Please don't cry.

Beat.

What am I doing? Whoever you are, if you ever call here again, I'll fuckin' kill you!!

> *ROGER slams down the phone. He runs over to J.C. and grabs him by the collar.*

Who was that?!

J.C.   All those fibre optics and you couldn't tell who it was? It was your mother. Dead all these years and when she finally calls, you yell at her. Ever dumb.

ROGER Dead people don't call you on the telephone.

J.C.   Well, aren't you a smartie pants. Dead people can do whatever they want. They're spirits. You gonna tell a spirit it can't call you? Good luck.

ROGER Mary. Get the door.

MARY Roger...

ROGER Open the goddamn door! I'm throwing this asshole out.

> *MARY goes to the door.*

MARY This is why we never have any visitors!

> *MARY struggles with the door, it will not budge.*

ROGER What's wrong?

MARY It's stuck.

> *ROGER goes to the door and tries to open it. It still won't open. ROGER goes back to J.C.*

ROGER What did you do to our door?

J.C.   Nothing.

> *The door swings open, by itself.*

ROGER *(taken aback)* Okay...? Good. Now get out.

> *The door slams shut. The lights flicker on and off. The door repeatedly opens and closes. Suddenly, it stops. J.C. is giggling to himself.*

J.C.   If you could see the looks on your faces...

MARY   Who are you!

J.C.   If I told you, you wouldn't believe it.

ROGER   Try us.

J.C.   I go by the name J.C, but I'm called different things by differ-
          ent cultures. Since you're both First Nations, I'll put it to you
          like this—I'm a Trickster. If you wanted to get specific you
          could call me Coyote.... But that's a little cliché, don't you
          think?

          Beat.

ROGER   Are you on crack?

J.C.   Not at all.

ROGER   Are you on a day pass?

J.C.   I'm not crazy, either. Or maybe I am. Who's to say what's
          crazy, and what's sane?

ROGER   Well, chances are, if you have to ask.... Listen, J.C.... I don't
          know how you did the shit with the door, and the lights, and
          the phone call, and quite frankly, I really don't care. I want
          you to go. So if you'll just grab your coat... or should I say,
          pelt... and exit out...

          *The lights flicker on and off. The door opens and closes.
          The phone rings. All of these things happen, louder, and
          much more violently, this time. MARY clings to ROGER.*

MARY   All right!! Enough!!

          It stops.

J.C.   Pretty cool, eh?

MARY   Why are you doing this?

J.C.   I told you, Mary. My job is to change things. How are we
          gonna do that if you won't pay attention?

ROGER   This is bullshit. You're not a Trickster. Tricksters are folklore.
          They're stories. They're just a tool for teaching lessons.

J.C.   Roger, listen... I'm a Trickster. That was your mother on the
          phone. And I *am* here, to teach you a lesson. So if you'll both
          just sit down we can all get started.

No response.

I'm older than dust and I tire out easily. Don't make me chase you all over this apartment. Sit.... Please?

> *ROGER and MARY go to the couch, sit down, and wait.*
> *J.C. walks up behind them.*

Comfy?

> *They both nod.*

Good. Now, Sign.

> *He hands them the paperwork, and a pen. They start to*
> *sign the papers.*

Fasten your seatbelts kids. It's going to be a bumpy ride.

> *Blackout.*

II ii

> *The apartment. An hour later. The stage is in blackness.*
> *A single light comes up on ROGER.*

ROGER It was the coldest night of the winter. Or maybe I just remember it that way. I'd been home from school for hours. My parents still weren't there. That wasn't new. Normally, I would go to my Granny's house till they came to get me, their breath soaked with booze. Staggering with me, all the way home. The last few nights though, my Granny was at the hospital in town, with pneumonia. Mom and Dad didn't even go to visit her. Probably for the best. So, I was alone. I cleaned up for a bit—Dad always hated a dirty house. Just as I was dozing off to sleep, the car came roaring up.

> *Lights change. We see shadows of a couple fighting.*
> *ROGER becomes his parents.*

FATHER You're not going anywhere!

MOTHER Yes I am! I'm not coming back! I mean it this time!

FATHER   Where you gonna go? You gonna stay with the mechanic you've been fuckin' in town?

MOTHER   I ain't been with anybody, you son of a bitch! Where's Roger...? Roger...!? Get dressed! We're leaving.

FATHER   You're not taking him anywhere. Get away from that room, you slut!

Back to spotlight on ROGER.

ROGER   Just as the door opened, and the light from the living room filled my bedroom, it happened.

A loud gunshot is heard.

He reloaded the rifle.

Another loud gunshot is heard.

And silence. I crept to my door. Just outside my bedroom was my mother, face down, soaked with blood. My father kneeling over her. His face was streaked with tears. It was the only time I ever saw him cry. He looked up at me and said, "Roger. Come and say goodbye to Daddy." The next thing I remember was climbing out my bedroom window, and running through the snow in my bare feet. Down the hill, to the reserve. I never saw my father put the gun in his mouth, but I heard the shot as I was running. And I still hear it, every time I close my eyes to sleep. And every time I dream, I see every detail of that night, being played over and over again. Just like I'm watching it on a movie... Some endless, fuckin', movie.

Lights fade up. MARY and J.C. are sitting on the couch, listening. There is a pause, then—

MARY   You never talked about it before. I mean, gone into detail.

J.C.   I'm gonna go out on a limb here.... You got some Daddy issues, don't you?

ROGER   Just telling you how it happened. So, what was the point of all that? I hope you weren't expecting some cathartic moment.

J.C.   You needed to get it out.

ROGER   Oh, really? Why's that?

J.C. People like you go through life never talking about anything, building up emotion, till one day—Kaboom!! You're on the news being described as that quiet guy next door. People need to clean house every once in a while, to make room for the new stuff.

ROGER Even so... why do you care?

J.C. It's not just me, Roger. It's the whole group collective.

ROGER What group collective?

J.C. Everyone. Your mother. Your father. Buddha. Custer. The whole gang. All the swinging kids from the spirit world. They're all here.

ROGER Really? If I knew we were having company, I would have shaved.

J.C. Skeptic, eh? What's the matter? Don't you believe in spirits?

ROGER Of course. I have to. I'm Indian. If I don't, I get my status card taken away.

J.C. So, where do you think the spirit world is?

ROGER Twelfth Avenue. Just off Main Street. How should I know?

J.C. It's right here.

MARY In this apartment?

J.C. Yes. It's all around us. And in us.

ROGER May the force be with you.

J.C. This is Indian spirituality 101, people. Come on. Try to keep up. The spirit world and the physical world are one and the same. We're all part of a group collective. Get it?

   No response.

  Okay, let me put it this way—did you guys ever see "The Lion King"...?

MARY So, you're saying we're in the spirit world right now?

J.C. Think of the spirit world, as a big apartment building. And think of each apartment unit as an existence. Like any apartment building, the way you conduct your life in your unit is going to directly affect the rest of your building. If you're good tenants, you'll get more perks. If you always play the stereo too loud, and pee on the carpeting, the rest of the building won't be too happy with you. Not only that, but your carpet... will smell like pee.

ROGER   That's a pretty simplistic belief system.

J.C.   I like to think of your belief system as whatever gets you out of bed in the morning. That way there can never be any right or wrong beliefs.

ROGER   Well, I believe my father killing my mother was pretty fuckin' wrong.

J.C.   It would seem he does too. Otherwise, he wouldn't have aired out his melon. The way each of you dealt with the act is where the power of choice comes in. Up to this point, those choices have been a little squirrelly.

ROGER   Once again, why do you care?

J.C.   You're adding to the collective. That gets people excited. In with the new. We just don't want the arrival of Junior to be fraught with anger and resentment. It's bad for the collective.

ROGER   I think the jury's still out on that one.

MARY   I said, I have to think about things.

J.C.   Mary, what's more important to you in the long run? Career or family?

MARY   Why can't I have both?

J.C.   You can, but right now, you're being asked to choose.

MARY   I think it's important to be secure before having a family.

ROGER   That's not what you said last night.

J.C.   Roger, why does it bother you that she might be changing her mind? Is it like she said, you're afraid you might lose her?

ROGER   I think it's... inevitable.

MARY   Holy insecurity! Where are you getting this from?

ROGER   You didn't even blink when you heard about the part. Nothing else was a consideration.

MARY   So, what do you want me to say, Roger? Forget acting. I'll stay here. Have an abortion. Stand by my man. You are my king. Is that what you want to hear?

ROGER   Ideally? Sure. But I'm not saying don't have a career. Just do it here, so we can share it together.

MARY   What if you want to go somewhere else, someday? Do I follow you wherever you go?

ROGER   I would hope you would want to.

MARY   And I would. Why can't you do the same for me?

ROGER   Because…. It doesn't work that way… I'm the man.

MARY   What!?

J.C.   Oooooh, shit!

ROGER   Wait! That didn't come out right.

MARY   It sure as hell didn't!

ROGER   No, you misunderstood.

MARY   You don't want a wife at all. You want an appendage. Someone who will support you no matter what, but doesn't have a life of her own. Is that why you're with a Native woman?

ROGER   What?

MARY   I mean, you've made it very clear to me, how you feel about Native people, yet you're in a relationship with one.

ROGER   I'm in this relationship because I love you.

MARY   Oh yeah!? *(mocking ROGER)* How do you know?

ROGER   Mary you're blowing this way out of proportion.

MARY   Am I? I think you're with an Indian woman 'cause you think I'll just stand in the background, looking pretty, while you sit around the tee-pee telling stories about the buffalo hunt.

ROGER   J.C. Help me out here.

J.C.   You're on your own, buddy.

MARY   You got some twisted idea that I should be some demure little Indian maiden. That same image you pretend to be so disgusted by on television. You hypocrite. Well, you're right about one thing, that is the stereotype. I just didn't expect another Indian to fall for it.

ROGER   What does our being Indian have to do with any of this?

MARY   Back on the reserve, we were told to find a man, stand behind him, and bear him children. That was it. And you've never shaken that reserve mentality.

ROGER   Hey! You're the one that's always trying to get me to do things Indian way.

MARY   Yeah, but you've forgotten, that ain't Indian way. Before the Europeans, women were respected. Men protected the women and sought their opinion. They didn't own them. That's the problem Roger, you want to own me.

ROGER   That's not true.

MARY   Yes it is, and I'm sick of it. J.C. said we all gotta make choices. I'm choosing my future. Not what you want mine to be. My own future, and that starts with the present.

ROGER   What the hell are you talking about?

MARY   Well, presently, I'm the one with a financial future; I'm the one with the option to start a family. Looks like I'm the boss. Things are going to change, and you better change with 'em.

ROGER   Or what!? You'll leave me? We agreed, no more ultimatums!

MARY   This isn't an ultimatum, it's a promise. I've made my choice... I'm going to do the show.

ROGER   I don't believe this!

MARY   And... I'm keeping this baby.

ROGER   Excuse me?

MARY   I'm not telling anyone I'm pregnant, till I have to. They'll have to deal with it when I become obvious.

ROGER   They won't deal with it!

MARY   Tough. They can write me out. And that, my loving husband, is that. Ball's in your court.

>   *Beat.*

ROGER   *(to J.C.)* See what you've done?

MARY   No, Roger. This is what we've done. You were right, I was acting blind, but my eyes are open now. J.C. made me realise I have a choice. I'm not alone out there. I'm part of something bigger than the walls of this apartment.

ROGER   So, you've had an epiphany. Well Mare, it all sounds nice in theory, but just remember, you still have to go out into that big, bad world. You telling me you gonna do it without me?

MARY   No, Roger. That's what you're telling me.

ROGER   So, what are you going to do? Find someone who'll do it with you?

MARY   You know? For the first time, it doesn't matter to me if there's someone there or not. I'll be fine.

ROGER   You really believe that?

MARY   Sure. You know what else? Maybe I will find someone who wants to be with me and support my decisions. Why not? I can find someone like that. Look at me. I'm fuckin' hot!

ROGER   You're not going anywhere.

MARY   You just sounded like your father.

ROGER   You take that back.

MARY   Maybe you are on your way to being like him. If that's the case, the last thing in the world we can do is raise our child together.

ROGER   So you really think you've seen the light, eh? Well, I'll tell you something, Mary. Whatever you think you believe, you are still in the exact same position you were yesterday.

MARY   No, Roger. You are. Things are quite different for me today. I got a cheque. I got a new job. I got a child on the way. And I got a new friend.

     MARY smiles at J.C. Beat.

ROGER   I knew it. It all makes sense. You're leaving me because of him. Well, there you go. Turns out it's not me who's like my father, it's you. You're exactly like *your* father.

MARY   Roger, don't.

ROGER   So, I was right. First chance you get, you snag the first lay that comes along.

MARY   Roger, he's not even really... real.

ROGER   Jesus! You fell hook, line, and sinker for that bullshit. He's not a spirit. Don't you see what he was doing? He was trying to turn you against me, so he could have a crack at you. It was all part of his plan...

J.C.   What?

ROGER   ...Or maybe you didn't need convincing. Maybe you just have a tough time keeping your pants on. Like father, like daughter. Maybe all this time I was completely oblivious to the fact that you're just a dirty little slut.

MARY   What the fuck did you call me!?

ROGER   Hey! You know when you were a little girl and you walked in on your dad screwing another woman? What am I saying? Of course you do. That incident is legendary on our reserve...

MARY   Shut up.

ROGER   ...Who was the chick he was doing? Wouldn't that be something if it was my mom? What if he had to leave because you caught him fucking my mother? That would kind of make us related.

MARY   Shut your fuckin' mouth.

ROGER   And what if the only reason we got together was because fucking me would be a symbolic gesture of you being a whore, like your dad!

MARY   Roger, stop!

ROGER   Why Mary? Did I hit a nerve?

MARY   You want to know who it was?

ROGER   Do I ever.

MARY   Yeah? You really want to know?

ROGER   Sure.

MARY   It wasn't a woman. It was a little girl.

ROGER   What?

MARY   It was me.

>   *Beat.*

ROGER   Mary...

MARY   I was the one my father was caught with. Okay!? Happy!?

>   *Beat.*

ROGER   Mary, I'm sorry...

MARY   That's why my father left. Not because I caught him with another woman, because my mother caught him raping me.

ROGER   I didn't know.

MARY   She told everyone he was caught with another woman, to save me from the hell I would have to go through. After a while, we just sort of convinced ourselves that's what happened.

ROGER   You never told me.

MARY   You said my mother was choosing to be blind. Maybe you're right. Maybe she did know what was happening, and chose to ignore it. If she did, I could never forgive her, but if she didn't, well... I never told her what was happening! And don't try to tell me I didn't know any better. Kids grow up way too fast on our reserve not to know. I knew exactly what was happening, and I didn't say shit. I didn't say a single, fucking, thing! So, go ahead and call me filthy names, Roger. Take your best shot! 'Cause there isn't a single thing you could call me that I haven't already called myself.

ROGER   I was angry. I wouldn't have said those things if I knew.

MARY   So what? This changes everything now?

ROGER   I didn't know!

MARY   It doesn't matter, Roger. You said them. The one man, who was never even supposed to think something like that, said them.

ROGER   I was upset.

MARY Do you know how hard it was for me to trust you, or any man, after something like that? To open up to you, to have sex with you? And after all that, to be called a whore, and a slut.

ROGER I didn't mean it.

MARY How many other things didn't you mean, since we've been together...? Never mind. Don't answer that. It doesn't matter anymore. This is the last time I'll have to question you.

MARY goes to the closet and pulls out the suitcase she packed before. She heads for the door.

ROGER You're not serious!?

MARY I'm tired, Roger. Tired of pretending it's all gonna get better. It's not. There's a baby coming and I'm too tired to be strong for all of us.

ROGER This is ridiculous. Give me one more chance.

MARY If what J.C. says is true, you'll get your chance. And when that day comes, Roger, I hope I'll be able to understand how a guy so loved, so worthy of my love, would do everything in his power to make me hate him. 'Cause right now, I could never understand.

ROGER Mary, please. I love you!

MARY grabs the door handle and stops.

MARY I love you too, Roger. I always will. But now, I gotta start saying it to myself.

ROGER Wait...!

Beat.

...The door's stuck.

MARY turns the handle. The door opens. They both look at J.C.

J.C. How 'bout that.

She starts to leave. Suddenly, ROGER kicks the door shut.

ROGER Mary. Don't go.

MARY Roger, stop it.

ROGER   We have to talk about this.

MARY   Roger, quit making this harder than it has to be.

> *She opens the door. ROGER kicks it shut again. He grabs MARY by the arms and pulls her away from the door.*

ROGER   I'm not going to let you walk through that door, after everything we've been through.

MARY   Stop it!

J.C.   Roger! Let her go!

ROGER   *(to J.C.)* Stay out of this! *(He turns back to MARY.)* You can't leave. I need you.

MARY   Goddamn it, Roger!! You're hurting my arm!!

> *J.C. runs over and tries to get in between them.*

J.C.   That's enough!

> *He grabs ROGER and tries to pull him away from MARY.*

ROGER   GET THE FUCK OFF ME!!!

> *ROGER turns on J.C. and punches him in the stomach. J.C. goes down. In a fit of rage, ROGER starts to kick and punch him.*
>
> *The sound of traffic, sirens and various city noises, rises.*
>
> *MARY grabs ROGER and tries to pull him off. In the struggle, MARY is thrown to the ground.*
>
> *The city noises fade to silence.*
>
> *ROGER turns to MARY, realising what he has done.*

Mary! Are you okay!?

> *He moves to help her.*

MARY   Get away from me!

> *She gets to her feet.*

ROGER   Sweetheart. I'm sorry. It was an accident. Let me help you.

MARY   Don't touch me.

She runs to the bathroom, and locks the door. ROGER
turns to J.C. who is very casually brushing himself off.
Unfazed by the beating.

ROGER   This is all your fault!

J.C.   Me? You pushed her.

ROGER   It was an accident! None of this would have happened if you didn't come here, filling her head with that shit. We were doing fine, till you showed up.

J.C.   I don't know about that.

ROGER   We were working through it!

J.C.   Really? Looked to me like you were wallowing in self-pity... just a little.

ROGER   I was feeling bad about myself, but I never wanted her to leave.

J.C.   I think you just didn't expect her to leave.

ROGER   I never meant any of it. I never thought she'd be better off without me.

J.C.   You try to convince somebody of something long enough, pretty soon they're gonna believe it.

ROGER   This is what you wanted. You weren't here to help us patch things up. You were here to split us apart.

J.C.   Just trying to keep things interesting.

ROGER   You lied to us.

J.C.   What did you expect? I'm a Trickster. I change things. If you're starting to think about how your life is going, then good. Change it.

ROGER   You're a bastard.

J.C.   I yam, what I yam.

MARY comes out of the bathroom.

MARY   I'm bleeding.

ROGER   Where?

MARY   Where do you think!?

ROGER   You're spotting. It's natural when women first get pregnant. Right, J.C.? Women have spotting.

J.C.   Yes, they do.

MARY   I'm not spotting, I'm bleeding!

ROGER   Honey. It's natural. Tell her J.C.…. J.C.? Tell her.

J.C.   I'm very sorry, Mary.

MARY slumps down into the kitchen chair.

MARY   Oh my God.

ROGER   Mary… I…

MARY   Don't say you're sorry. Don't say anything to me ever again. You've lost that right.

ROGER   You have to let me help you get through this.

MARY   I think you've done enough.

J.C.   Mary, you can't blame Roger for this. Sometimes the body miscarries if something's not right. If the fall didn't do it, something else probably would have.

ROGER   There. You see? Neither one of us is to blame for this.

J.C.   On the other hand, maybe the fall did cause it. Who knows?

ROGER   You son of a bitch! Get out of our house!

MARY   Your house, Roger. I'm moving to Winnipeg. I'm going to be on television.

She starts to leave.

ROGER   Mary, wait…! I've changed. I know that. But I can change back to who I was. I can be the man you want me to be. Let me at least try. Please! Mary, I'm looking my future in the face right now, and all I can see is emptiness if you walk out that door.

MARY   I have to go, Roger.

ROGER   I'm begging you. Mary. Please. You're my everything.

MARY   No, Roger. The person you've become is not my responsibility, or my fault.

She picks up her suitcase.

Goodbye, Roger. Live your life well.

She quickly exits. ROGER watches her go. Beat. ROGER looks to J.C.

J.C.   Let her go.

ROGER turns and runs out to the street, where he spots MARY walking quickly and crying.

ROGER   MARY!!

MARY stops, and turns to ROGER. They hold each other's gaze for a long beat. ROGER fights back tears.

I wanted to give you the rest of the money, from the TV. I mean, it's yours anyway.

He hands the money to her. She takes it. ROGER, gently, takes her hand.

You didn't give me a chance to say... I mean... live your life well, Mary.

MARY   That's the first time I've ever seen you cry.

ROGER   It hurts like hell.

MARY   It's good for you.

MARY turns, and slowly walks off. ROGER watches her go. He goes and sits on the park bench. Beat. J.C. appears beside him.

ROGER   Am I ever going to see her again?

J.C.   Depends how bad you want it.

ROGER   Honestly.

J.C.   Probably not.

ROGER   Am I ever going to see you again?

J.C.   Probably not.

ROGER   Good.

J.C.   Well... not in this form, anyway.

ROGER   Aw... fuck.

J.C.   Oh, and one more thing. I hate to pile this on you now, but...
           I didn't pay your phone bill.

ROGER   What?

J.C.   Check it, when you go back inside. It's stone cold dead.

ROGER   What!?

J.C.   Hey. I'm a spirit. Where am I gonna get money to pay a
           phone bill?

ROGER   You mean, those cheques you gave us...?

J.C.   Oh no. Those are real. Think of it as starting over money.

ROGER   The call from my mother...?

J.C.   That was real, too. You don't need a working phone to call
           someone, when you're a spirit. Membership has its privileges.

ROGER   Mary's acting job?

J.C.   Well...

ROGER   No!?

J.C.   In the great tradition of the film industry—they gave the part
           of the Indian wife, to an Italian girl. The role was cast over a
           month ago.

ROGER   How could you do that!? She's out there all alone!

J.C.   She's not alone.

ROGER   Well, she's out there thinking she has a great, film role! Why
           would you do that to her!?

J.C.   Good question—Story time!

ROGER   Aw fuck. Why'd I ask?

J.C.   A hungry hawk comes across a snake, sitting at the edge of a
           canyon. Just as the hawk is about to strike, the snake shouts,
           "Don't eat me! Carry me across the canyon and I'll take you
           to my brothers and sisters. You'll feast for days." "If I car-
           ried you, why wouldn't you poison me and eat me first?" the

questioning hawk… questions. "Silly bird, if I poison you we'll both fall and die," retorts the snake. So the hawk picks up the snake in it's claws and starts across the canyon…

ROGER   Let me guess. Halfway through the flight, the snake bites him. Right?

J.C.   Bang on, sparky! The snake's venom paralyses the hawk. As the two plunge to their deaths, the hawk cries out, "Why!?" To which the snake replies, "I'm a snake. It's in my nature."

ROGER   And you're a Trickster.

J.C.   It's in my nature. Thing is, Roger, you both made choices. Those choices changed things. Hopefully, for the better. That's all any of us can hope for.

ROGER   But, Mary…

J.C.   Mary's gonna be fine, and so will you. You're off to a good start. Things will work out in the end. They always do.

ROGER   I guess…. Well, J.C, I guess I better get back home. I'd like to say it's been fun… unfortunately…

J.C.   Understood.

> ROGER starts to leave.

Hey, Roger! You're a good kid. Remember…. You're the only you, you got.

> ROGER turns and heads for home. J.C. watches him go. Lights fade down to focus on J.C. He turns to the audience.

Gather 'round brothers and sisters. Huddle together underneath this artificial light and seek solace amongst your people. Darkness is falling once again across this city and we are all strangers in this foreign land. Some of you look familiar. Some of you I have yet to meet. Whichever you are, mark my words; what seems like logic is only illusion.

> Spotlights come up on ROGER and MARY. ROGER is in the apartment, sitting at the desk. MARY is sitting on a park bench.

As for these two lost souls? I'd like to say... they made out fine. Mary became successful in film and theatre, and Roger went on to publish a string of novels. All in all—I would like to say—things worked out, in the end.

Beat.

I would like to say that.... But.... Then again.... Maybe it didn't.

Lights fade on J.C. as he walks offstage. Lights fade on MARY. Lights fade on ROGER.

Blackout.

The end.

Darrell Dennis is a First Nations writer from the Shuswap Nation in the interior of British Columbia. His short stories have been published in periodicals across the country. His work has also been broadcast nationally on CBC radio. Darrell is a produced playwright and an award-winning writer for television. His script "Moccasin Flats" was an official selection at the 2003 Sundance Film Festival and was later turned into a series for the Showcase Network. His one man show, *Tales of an Urban Indian* was nominated for two Dora Mavor Moore Awards: "Outstanding New Play" and "Outstanding Performance by a Male." Darrell is currently working on a novel, a collection of short stories, a feature film script, and is writing for several television series'. In addition, Darrell is a full time student at the University of Toronto where he received a National Scholarship and is working towards an Honours degree in English and Aboriginal Studies.